MANHATTAN'S DESSERT SCENE

NEW YORK CITY'S TOP DESSERT SPOTS
REVEAL THEIR SECRET RECIPES

ROSE REISMAN

Published by Lymas Publications Ltd.

Canadian Cataloguing in Publication Data

Reisman, Rose, 1953-
    Manhattan's Dessert Scene
Includes index

ISBN 0-9693365-1-9
1. Desserts 2. Restaurants, lunch rooms, etc.
 Manhattan–New York I. Title
 (TX 773. R44 1989   641.8'6   088-893315-1)

Printed by Friesen Printers
Altona, Manitoba

Design: Don Fernley
Photography: Richard Allan
Front Cover Dessert: Quilted Giraffe—White and Dark Chocolate Marbled
                Mousse Cake: prepared by Sitram Sharma,
                Four Seasons Inn on the Park
Props: Rose Reisman
Front Cover Props Assistant: Carol Takasaki
Writing: Nancy Kilpatrick/Rose Reisman
Editorial: Nancy Kilpatrick
Proofreading: Christine Hebscher

Typeset by Menesetung Enterprises Incorporated
45 Woodlawn Avenue West
Toronto, Ontario, Canada

Printed in Canada

Distributed in Canada by MacMillan of Canada
                29 Birch Avenue
                Toronto, Ontario, M4V 1E2
                Call collect (416) 293–2020

Distributed in United States by Independent Publishing Group
                814 N. Franklin St.
                Chicago, IL 60610
                Order toll-free (800) 888–4741

Published by Lymas Publications Ltd. (Toronto)

DEDICATION

I dedicated my first book, *The Dessert Scene —Toronto's Top Dessert Spots Reveal Their Secret Recipes,* to my husband. As another year has passed, I feel that I must dedicate this New York book to my best friend, supporter, taste tester and most important critic—my husband!

All of the desserts had careful input given by the tiny tasting hands of my three blessings, Natalie, David and our newest family member, Laura lovely, to whom I also dedicate this book.

Rose Reisman

Contents

RAINBOW ROOM *59*
Frozen Praline Soufflé with Chocolate Sauce /
Baked Alaska with Fruit Sauce

LE CIRQUE *62*
Crisp Millefeuille with Fresh Fruit / Crème Brûlée

LE CYGNE *65*
Chocolate Mousse Roulade /
Raspberry Mousse with Strawberry Sauce /
Strawberry and Kiwi Cream Tart

LA RÉSERVE *69*
Tarte Tartin / Hazelnut Buttercream Cake with Anise

GOTHAM BAR AND GRILL *72*
Vanilla Poached Pears with Figs and Apricots /
Five Fruit and Berry Compote / Classic Crème Brûlée

AURORA *76*
Apple Tart / Fresh Berries with Granite of Pinot Noir /
Apricot Mousse

LAFAYETTE *80*
Mango Strudel with Kiwi Sauce / Passion Fruit Mousse Cake /
Vanilla Pears with Cherry Sauce

LA TULIPE *84*
Lemon Chiffon Tart / Apricot Soufflé /
Tulipe Cookie Cups filled with Ice Cream and Chocolate Sauce

FRASER MORRIS *88*
Lemon and Lime Meringue Pie /
Espresso Chocolate Mousse Charlotte /
Fraser Morris's Famous Rice Pudding /
Baked Apples with Almond Cream

LES DÉLICES GUY PASCAL *93*
Orange and Chocolate Layered Mousse Cake /
Swiss Ganache Cake

MISS GRIMBLE'S *97*
Chocolate Texas Pecan Torte / Miss Grimble's ABC Cheesecake /
Apple Raisin Tart

LE BERNARDIN   *102*
> Anise Ice Cream with Coffee Sauce /
> Fruit "Soup" with Orange Cream

JOHN CLANCY'S   *105*
> Chocolate Cream Roulade / Mocha Crème Brûlée /
> Bourbon Pecan Tart / Almond Pear Cream Tart

PEPPERMINT PARK   *112*
> Apple Nut Cake with Cream Cheese Glaze /
> Peppermint Stick Ice Cream / Double Chocolate Chunk Cookies /
> Chocolate Lovers' Chocolate Sundae

CHALET SUISSE   *117*
> Chocolate Dacquoise Layered with Cream and Berries /
> Hollander Cake / Swiss Chocolate Fondue / Classic Bread Pudding

FERRARA   *122*
> Cream Puffs with Cannoli Filling and Chocolate Sauce /
> Almond Ricotta Cheesecake

GINDI   *125*
> Chocolate and Coffee Truffle Cake / Chocolate Pecan Pie /
> Sour Cream Apple Pie

SARABETH'S KITCHEN   *129*
> Rugelach / Chocolate Chip Almond Cookies / Sarabeth's Scones

BETWEEN THE BREAD   *133*
> Walnut Lemon Butter Tart / Pear and Puff Pastry Tart /
> Chocolate Hazelnut Cake

Biography

Rose Reisman is a 35-year-old dessert aficionado with twelve years' experience as a self-taught baker. Whether it's writing a cookbook, or relaxing with friends and family, her unbridled love for desserts finds her preparing desserts at any time of the day or night. She's able to maintain her petite figure by adhering to her philosophy that the finest quality dessert is best appreciated when consumed in small amounts.

Rose holds two post-graduate degrees, (M.B.A. and M.F.A.) from York University, and most recently, taught business courses at Seneca College. In 1988 she published her first cookbook, *The Dessert Scene – Toronto's Top Dessert Spots Reveal Their Secret Recipes*, and the book's success has prompted the publication of a second edition.

Her second book, *Manhattan's Dessert Scene*, features more of the world's greatest desserts and is a collaborative effort with some of New York's renowned chefs and establishments.

Rose resides in Toronto with her husband and three young children.

Acknowledgments

Flowers donated by Bay Flowers in Toronto.
Tableware donated by Villeroy and Boch Tableware Ltd. in Toronto.
Materials donated by B.B. Bargoon's in Toronto.

All of the desserts prepared for the photographs were produced by the Toronto Four Seasons Inn on the Park's pastry chef, Sitram Sharma. The decorations are Mr. Sharma's own artistic interpretation of the New York chefs' recipes. The actual desserts in each of the establishments may have a different appearance.

A word about Sitram is in order. Born in Guyana, he came to Canada in 1981. He worked at several of Toronto's top hotels as pastry chef, until he decided to remain at the exclusive Four Seasons Inn on the Park, as executive pastry chef, where he has been for close to two years.

The Four Seasons presents a great challenge for someone as creative and dynamic as Sitram. His love and expertise lie in chocolate and sugar work, and he has won gold medals at food and wine shows for his spectacular creations.

I am ever so grateful for his wonderful participation in *Manhattan's Dessert Scene*.

Introduction

Two years ago, my life-long passion for desserts propelled me into a wild and wonderful adventure.

Up to that point, I had baked at home for over twelve years, studying from international pastry chefs of well-known and lesser-known repute, perfecting my skills and unearthing luscious dessert recipes in the process. My adoration for baking often keeps me in the kitchen until all hours preparing simple, homey goodies or exquisitely decadent creations. Fortunately, I discovered an important secret for anyone who can't resist the seductive sweets—small portions of top quality desserts are far more satisfying than larger portions of mediocre fare. That philosophy, combined with an adoration of those skilled in this art, inspired my search for excellence in desserts.

I have always dreamed about the experience of collaborating with world-class pastry chefs to produce a cookbook which would incorporate personal touches and hints guaranteed to yield the same spectacular results as those exotic treats we yearn for, available at only the finest of establishments. What I envisioned was a sampling of the world's best dessert recipes, written with home bakers in mind. Since I couldn't find such a book, I decided that the opportunity was at hand.

In 1987, when I embarked on *The Dessert Scene*, a collection of recipes from Toronto's finest pastry spots, I had no idea it would be such a runaway success. The first edition sold out in three months and a revised second edition is in print.

Last year, I set a new goal—an impossible dream. Could I put together recipes created by the great dessert chefs of New York? The task of selecting from literally hundreds of eateries was daunting; convincing famous chefs to share their secrets seemed an insurmountable challenge. Being seven months pregnant at the time just added another hurdle to this endeavour. Incredibly, I convinced the likes of Barry Wine (Quilted Giraffe) and André Soltner (Lutèce) to be two of 29 fabulous eateries to participate in *Manhattan's Dessert Scene*. This focused and informative book has 100 of the formerly best-kept New York treasures. Each of the 100 recipes has been carefully adapted for home baking without comprising quality or taste. I personally tested and retested every dessert and can offer assurance that they are not only easy to make, but the results will astonish both you and your guests.

For my next venture, I'm off to exciting California to collect recipes for *The West Coast Dessert Scene*. In the meantime, I hope you will enjoy this compilation of Manhattan's best desserts, now exposed for the first time. *Bon appetit!*

Helpful Hints
to Achieve Perfect Results
with the Following Recipes

Please, no matter how competent a baker you are, read this brief section careful-ly. It is well worth the time.

Chocolate Melting – Break into smaller pieces and melt in a microwave under defrost for 2-4 minutes, depending on the quantity. You can also use a double boiler over simmering heat. Transfer melted chocolate into new bowl and let cool slightly before adding eggs, whipping cream, liquors, or whipped egg whites.

Chocolate Curls – use a vegetable peeler, cheese slicer or sharp knife. Hold chocolate chunk in hands for a few minutes to soften. Peel chocolate, turning it around in your hands when one side starts to melt. Store curls in a cool place.

Gelatin – one package equals one tablespoon. Gelatin should be dissolved by first covering with cold water, approximately 1/4 cup. Let this rest one minute, then add 1/4 cup hot water. Stir until melted.

Layering Cakes – For cakes of more than two layers, inbetween frosting is made easier if layers are placed into the correct size of a springform pan and iced in the pan just before topping or sides are done. Place in freezer for a few minutes until set, remove springform and ice the tops and sides. This prevents icing from sliding out from sides.

Testing Cakes for Doneness – All cake recipes give approximate baking times because ovens, pans and measurements can differ. The non-stick pans can need as much as 25% less baking time. Therefore, ten minutes before the given recipe time is up, cakes should be tested by inserting a toothpick or tester into the middle. If wet, keep checking at 5 minute intervals. Sometimes a little bit of wetness in the middle will yield a moister cake.

Pecan Pies and Cheesecakes – These differ from other cakes because, needing to be moist, a small portion of the centre will remain loose.

Whipping Cream and Whipping Egg Whites – All cream and egg whites must be cold, fresh and whipped in clean, dry bowls in order to achieve the proper stiffness. If the bowl is wet or has any hint of foreign particles in it, then the cream and egg whites will never beat properly. Whip only until stiff peaks are reached. Over-beating cream will result in a curdled consistency.

Fresh and Frozen Fruit Purées – Usually 1 1/2 cups of fresh fruit will yield approximately 3/4 cup of purée, but always measure. When using frozen fruit, defrost and then be sure to strain the excess liquid before puréeing.

Food Processor – If a food processor is used to mix cakes or cookies, keep this in mind: after the flour has been added, use on-off motions to combine flour with other ingredients. Over-beating of flour results in a dry cake or cookie.

Molds – To invert, dip the bottom of the mold into a larger pan filled with boiling water for 5 seconds. Invert onto serving dish. If unsuccessful, try another 2-3 seconds. Note that if the mold is kept in the water too long, the ingredients will melt.

Parchment Paper – The greatest non-stick paper ever invented. When a recipe calls for this paper, butter and flour the paper to guarantee 100% success. This paper can be bought in grocery stores or specialty cooking stores. It can also be reused.

Garnishes

You don't have to be an expert pastry chef. Using basics can achieve spectacular results.

Confectioners' sugar or cocoa – Sift over cake.

Strawberries - Decorate with sliced strawberries.

Chocolate-glazed Strawberries – Melt 3 oz of chocolate with 1/2 tsp vegetable oil and dip half of strawberry with fork or toothpick into chocolate. Refrigerate until hardened on wax paper.

Jelly Glazes – Used to give fruit a sheen. Melt 2 tbsp and brush over fruit.

Nuts – Toast in oven on cookie sheet at 450°F or in dry pot over high heat on stove, until golden brown. Grind into desired texture.

Chocolate Glaze (Ganache) – Melt chocolate and measure whipping cream to equal half the amount of chocolate. Add cream and blend. Usually 4 oz of chocolate will glaze top of cake. Therefore use 2 oz of cream.

Substitutions

The real product is always the best, but in a crisis use these substitutes.

Butter – If butter is not the main ingredient, then substituting margarine, vegetable shortening or lard is acceptable. In desserts where butter is the main ingredient, for example pound cakes, substitutions may alter the taste greatly.

Sour cream – For a lighter version, substitute unflavored yogurt or buttermilk. Sour cream has a higher fat content and will produce a richer dessert.

Cheese – If cheesecakes call for cream cheese, substitute solid cottage cheese that has been well drained. A lighter, less creamy version will be produced.

Chocolate – Cocoa can be subtituted but the flavor will not be as rich. 1 oz of semi-sweet chocolate can be replaced with 1 tbsp sugar, 2 1/2 tsp butter and 1 1/2 tbsp cocoa.

Cream – Whipping cream or heavy cream and crème fraîche can all be substituted for one another. If light cream is needed, these heavy creams can also be substituted by diluting the heavy cream with half the amount of water. Do not substitute heavy cream for lighter creams. They will not whip nor thicken in the same way.

Sugar – Brown and white sugar can be substituted for one another. For each 1 cup of white or brown sugar, 2 cups of icing sugar is needed; 7/8 of a cup of honey or 1 1/4 cups of corn syrup can be used, as long as the liquid is reduced by 1/4 cup or the flour is increased by 1/4 cup.

LIST OF NECESSARY AND/OR HELPFUL EQUIPMENT

Food processor – Great for grinding, beating and mixing. Be sure to avoid overprocessing. Do not use for whipping egg whites or cream unless you have a special attachment.

Electric beater – Use for whipping, creaming, beating or stirring. Gives greater volume to eggs, butter and sugar.

Springform pans – This is a deep cake pan that has a removable side. Small, medium and large are all good to have on hand, plus a 9" size.

Large cake pans - 8" to 9" round pans are useful, especially when lined with parchment paper. A springform pan can replace a cake pan when greater depth is needed.

Bundt or tube pans – Useful for pound, fruit and coffee cakes—10" is the most common size. Always butter and flour.

Decorative mold pans (2-4 cup) – Good for mousses.

Jelly roll pans – Useful for sponge recipes. Line with buttered and floured parchment paper. Usual size is 15" x 10".

Bain-marie – Custard-type desserts or crustless cheesecakes at times require a bain-marie, or water-bath. A larger pan than the baking dish is filled halfway with simmering water. This method ensures the dessert will remain creamy and smooth. Do not put a springform pan in a water-bath, for it will leak.

TAVERN ON THE GREEN

Tavern On The Green is a legend in The Big Apple. Located at Central Park and West 67th Street, the restaurant features an eclectic menu, served amid enthralling fairytale splendor.

In warm weather, diners are permitted on the terrace where the trees, carefully spaced among garden tables and chairs, are swathed in twinkling lights. A visit to Tavern On The Green encapsules why people come to New York: a breathtaking evening view of Central Park; paths illuminated by quaint lighting; the sight of horses drawing mock-Victorian carriages; the rhythm of this energetic metropolis after dark.

Indoors are several dining rooms, including the famous Crystal Room. Multi-colored chandeliers suspended from a rococo ceiling, sparkling Venetian chandeliers and an astonishing 350,000 dazzling lights create the effect of an enchanting winter palace. The cosier Chestnut Room is available for intimate dinners.

Cuisine ranges from trendy to traditional, hot to cold dishes. Because this establishment is perennially popular and caters to such a diverse clientele, everyone finds something that will appeal to the appetite.

A selection of fantastic desserts includes Chocolate Macadamia Nut Cake, a tribute to Hawaii's best; an Iced Lemon Soufflé that will thrill guests; and the elegant White Chocolate Mousse Layer Cake with Raspberries, an exquisite dream.

White Chocolate Mousse Layer Cake With Raspberries

Preheat oven to 350°F.
9" springform pan buttered and floured.

Chocolate Sponge

3 egg yolks 1/4 cup sugar	Beat until light in color.
1 tsp vanilla	Add and blend.
1 1/2 tbsp cocoa 1 tbsp flour	Fold into above, mixing gently. Set aside.
3 egg whites	Whip in clean bowl until soft peaks form.
1/4 cup sugar	Add to whites and beat until stiff. Fold into above cocoa/sugar mixture. Pour into pan and bake approximately 20 minutes, or until tester comes out clean. Cool on rack.

White Chocolate Mousse

10 oz white chocolate	Melt and stir until smooth.
3 egg yolks	Beat until blended. Mix into chocolate mixture. Set aside.
1 1/2 cups whipping cream	In clean bowl beat until soft peaks form. Set aside.
3 egg whites 1 tbsp sugar	In clean bowl beat until stiff. Fold cream and whites into chocolate/yolk mixture until blended.
1 pint raspberries	Set aside.

White Chocolate Mousse Layer Cake with Raspberries (continued)

Assembly

Slice sponge cake in 2 layers. Leave one layer in pan. Pour $1/3$ mousse over bottom cake. Scatter $1/2$ of the raspberries over top. Place second layer of cake over top. Place $1/3$ more mousse over cake. Chill remaining mousse. Chill cake for at least 2 hours. Unmold springform and ice sides with remaining chilled mousse. Decorate with raspberries or with large white chocolate shavings.

Chocolate Shavings

Soften 1 large piece of white chocolate by rotating it in your hands for several minutes. Use a knife or vegetable peeler to make large shavings.

White chocolate mousse along with chocolate sponge cake makes this dessert elegant and exquisite.

Chocolate Macadamia Nut Cake
(or any nut of your choice)

Preheat oven to 375°F.
Butter and flour 9" - 10" springform pan.

5 oz semi-sweet chocolate	Melt and stir until smooth. Set aside.
5 oz butter	Cream until fluffy.
4 egg yolks	Add to butter one at a time and beat until creamy. Add melted chocolate and mix well.
4 egg whites } $^1/_3$ cup sugar }	Beat in clean bowl until stiff. Fold into above chocolate mixture until whites disappear.
5 oz finely ground nuts (macadamia, almond, etc.)	Fold into above. Pour into pan and bake 25-30 minutes or until toothpick comes out clean. Cool on rack. Refrigerate and sift icing sugar over top. Serve at room temperature with Crème Anglaise. (Optional)

Crème Anglaise

2 egg yolks } $^1/_4$ cup sugar }	Beat in bowl until pale yellow. Set aside.
1 cup 10% or 18% cream	Heat in saucepan to just before boiling. Pour a little into yolk mixture and pour back into remaining cream. Stir constantly on low heat until thick, approximately 10-15 minutes. Do not let boil. Remove from heat.
1 tsp vanilla	Add and mix. Chill.

Macadamias are the richest nuts ever.
This cake is out of this world.

White Chocolate Mousse Layer Cake, pages 14 and 15

Iced Lemon Soufflé

6 cup mold or   Recipe can be cut in half
6 individual dishes

1 tsp gelatin	Dissolve according to package instructions until melted.
1/2 cup lemon juice (approx. 1 1/2 lemons)	Add to gelatin mixture. Set aside.
1 cup egg whites (approx. 7 large eggs)	Beat in clean bowl until foamy.
1 cup sugar	Add to whites and continue beating until glossy and sugar is dissolved. Set aside.
1 cup heavy cream	Whip in clean bowl until stiff. Fold whites and whipped cream into lemon juice mixture. Pour into mold, or dishes. Freeze until solid. If using mold, invert by placing pan in hot water for a few seconds.

*A frozen dessert that leaves a wonderful taste
after any meal.*

*Also great if served with strawberry sauce
(see page 67).*

Apple Cream Pie, page 27

"the Quilted Giraffe"

The name, The Quilted Giraffe, evokes a marvelous image. And there's no doubt about it; this spectacularly innovative restaurant caters to a sophisticated and discriminating clientele who can appreciate the unique.

After several incarnations, The Quilted Giraffe recently moved into an elegant space on Madison Avenue, and has settled comfortably into its spectacular new location at the American Telephone and Telegraph building. Hand-selected Japanese crockery enhances each serving; drink is served in Hoya crystal stemware. A two-tiered environment utilizes the quietest gray leather for banquettes and chairs. Jean Dubuffet prints hang on pastel walls, flowers adorn tables and candlelight illuminates it all.

Ambience aside, what springs immediately to mind about The Quilted Giraffe is, as it should be, the food itself. Owners Susan and Barry Wine, neither of whom is a classically trained restaurateur—Barry was a lawyer—aren't afraid to be inventive. The menu offers many one-of-a-kind creations, whimsically improvised in a surprisingly egalitarian kitchen. Dishes are carefully grilled or sautéed with both quality and freshness the priorities. The Quilted Giraffe may be New York's best restaurant. It certainly vies for most expensive. But the Wines take such pains with ingredients and presentation that the cost of a meal, for those who can afford it, becomes superfluous.

Desserts are the pinnacle of a nearly spontaneous menu. The Wines, who seem to enjoy delighting their customers, even offer a Grand Dessert, a sampling of every sweet available on any particular evening. But there are cheerfully simple desserts that contrast with the elaborate. Blueberry Crumple with Vanilla Ice Cream, Peach and Cherry Oatmeal Crisp and Vanilla Custard with Meringue Cookies are unforgettable delectables. Also, one must try the incredible front cover White and Dark Chocolate Marbled Mousse Cake.

Blueberry Crumple with Vanilla Ice Cream

Preheat oven to 375°F.
Butter and flour 1 cookie sheet.

Serves 6 to 8.

Blueberry Filling

2 cups blueberries
zest of $^{1}/_{2}$ lemon
$^{1}/_{2}$ cinnamon stick
$^{1}/_{4}$ cup water
$^{1}/_{4}$ cup sugar

Place in saucepan. Simmer until liquid is thick.
Remove zest and cinnamon stick then purée.

$^{1}/_{4}$ cup butter

Whisk in butter.

2 cups whole blueberries

Add to above. Set aside.

Crumple

5 filo pastry sheets

3 tbsp butter

Melt and brush lightly over each sheet of filo. Pile all five sheets on top of each other.

2 tbsp honey
1 tbsp white wine

Melt and brush lightly over top sheet. Do not soak filo.

$^{1}/_{2}$ cup finely ground toasted almonds
$^{1}/_{4}$ cup sugar

Sprinkle over honey mixture.

Place blueberry filling over top sheet. Roll up filo like a jelly roll, and bake until golden, approx. 20-25 minutes. Sprinkle with icing sugar. Serve with vanilla ice cream.

Filo pastry and warm blueberries can be a breakfast, snack or dinner delight.

White and Dark Chocolate Marbled Mousse Cake

12" springform pan.

Crust

1 cup chocolate wafers 3 tbsp melted butter }	Combine and pat into bottom of pan. Refrigerate while preparing filling.

Chocolate Filling

14 oz semi-sweet chocolate	Melt and stir until smooth.
2 eggs	Add and mix until well combined.
4 egg yolks	Add and mix until smooth. Set aside.
2 cups whipping cream	Whip in clean bowl until soft peaks form.
4 egg whites	Whip in clean bowl until stiff. Set aside. Alternately fold whites and cream into above chocolate mixture until well combined. Pour into crust. Set aside.

White Chocolate Mousse

2 1/2 oz white chocolate	Melt and stir until smooth.
2 egg yolks	Beat until blended. Mix into above chocolate mixture. Set aside.
1/2 cup whipping cream	In clean bowl beat until soft peaks form. Set aside.

White and Dark Chocolate
Marbled Mousse Cake
(continued)

White Marble (continued)

2 egg whites	In clean bowl beat until stiff. Fold cream and whites into chocolate/ yolk mixture until blended. Slowly pour into center of dark chocolate mousse. With a knife swirl white mousse a few times through chocolate. Chill for 3-4 hours.

This spectacular dessert can be served alone like this,
or with the decoration illustrated on the front cover.

Front Cover Decoration
(prepared by Sitram Sharma)

Measure height of cake. Take parchment paper and draw a band on paper, longer than cake circumference, and the identical height. 2–3 shorter bands are possible as well. Place bands on buttered cookie sheet. Melt 3 oz of white chocolate. With a pastry tube draw white lines, as on cover, on parchment band. Refrigerate until set. Melt 5 oz of compound dark chocolate and 1 tsp of oil. Pour a thin layer over white stripes and with a knife spread over bands of paper. Let set. Carefuly lift parchment band and wrap around cake. Let set. Remove parchment paper.

Chocolate Rolls

1 large piece of compound white chocolate 1 large piece of compound dark chocolate	Slightly soften each piece just until a sharp knife can be used to shave rolls similar to those on the front cover. Lay out as in photo. (Soften chocolate by rotating pieces in your hands for several minutes.)

Peach and Cherry Oatmeal Crisp

Preheat oven to 375°F.
8" baking dish.

Syrup

1 cup water 1 cup sugar $1/3$ cup Marsala wine $1/2$ squeezed lemon	Cook in saucepan for 10 minutes. Cool.
4 large firm peaches	Slice each of the 4 peaches into $1/8$th pieces. Marinate in above syrup while preparing topping.
1 very ripe peach (for purée)	Purée with $1/4$ of the above syrup. Set aside.
1 cup pitted fresh cherries	Set aside.

Crisp Topping

$3/4$ cup flour $3/4$ cup rolled oats 1 cup brown sugar	Combine in food processor.
4 oz chilled butter cut into cubes	Add to above until roughly incorporated. Small lumps of butter will still be evident.

Assembly

Spread peach purée on bottom of baking dish. Remove peach slices from syrup and arrange with cherries over purée. Cover with crisp topping. Bake approx. 20-25 minutes until topping is golden.

Great with ice cream or whipped cream!

Vanilla Custard with
Chocolate Meringue Cookies

Preheat oven to 325°F.
4–6 oven-proof individual dishes.

Custard

2 cups heavy cream ⎫ ¹/₄ cup sugar (125 ml) ⎭	Warm in saucepan until dissolved.
4 egg yolks ⎫ ¹/₄ cup sugar ⎭	Combine until creamy. In a clean bowl combine warm cream mixture with yolks. Stir. Pour into individual baking dishes. Bake in water-bath until set, approx. 35 minutes. Refrigerate until cold. Serve alone or with chocolate meringue cookies.

Chocolate Meringue Cookies

Preheat oven to 300° F.   Makes approx. 10 cookies
Line cookie sheet with buttered and floured parchment paper.

1 ³/₄ oz almonds	Grind in processor until very fine.
³/₄ tbsp cocoa ⎫ ¹/₂ tsp flour ⎬ ¹/₄ cup icing sugar ⎭	Sift into bowl. Add almonds.
1 egg white ⎫ 2 tbsp sugar ⎭	Beat in clean bowl until soft peaks form. Mix with above dry ingredients, just until combined. Pipe into 3" sticks or form with small teaspoon. Bake 20 minutes.

*This baked custard provides a wonderful contrast
to these light chocolate cookies.
Use both recipes together or have them separate.*

Chocolate Cream Soufflé

Preheat oven to 425°F.
Butter 6 individual soufflé dishes and sprinkle with sugar.

2 oz semi-sweet chocolate ⎫ 2 oz butter ⎬	Melt. Whisk until smooth. Set aside.
3 egg yolks ⎫ 1/4 cup warm water ⎬	Beat until light and foamy, approx. 3-4 minutes. Set aside.
6 egg whites	Beat until foamy in clean bowl.
1/3 cup sugar	Add to whites. Beat until firm peaks form. Combine yolk and chocolate mixtures. Carefully fold in whites until combined. Pour into dishes and bake 10–12 minutes. Remove from oven when soufflés are slightly wobbly and tops are brown. Cut tops open and serve with whipped cream or chocolate sauce.

Chocolate Sauce

3 oz semi-sweet chocolate	Melt and stir until smooth.
3/4 cup whipping cream	Add gradually and blend.

This soufflé is rich and creamy as well as being as easy as ABC!

Lutèce

Remarks frequently heard en passant from diners as they leave the famous Lutèce are *magnifique* and *extraordinaire*. With good reason. Long considered New York's premier restaurant, the one by which all others are measured, Lutèce quality and natural elegance are legendary and the cuisine has been reassuringly consistent for close to three decades.

André Soltner, chef-proprietaire, is nearly single-handedly responsible for an atmosphere of refinement in which exceptional dishes are offered with reverence. His approach in the kitchen is inexhaustibly exploratory, recognized by the fact that he is the recipient of all major culinary awards. The beautifully written menu at Lutèce, sans prices, rarely alters, but Soltner makes frequent trips from oven to table, attired in kitchen whites and toque blanche, informing diners of an abundance of unlisted, exceptional creations that are available.

Lutèce is the name by which Paris was known prior to the fourth century. There is an unassuming style here, built on charm and grace, a tribute to the birthplace of French gastronomy that introduces visitors to a simpler, more gracious way of life. This establishment is located in a townhouse with a French stone facade and is identified by a discreet gold and black sign. Once past the foyer and bar, as diners are led down a hallway they peek into the bustling kitchen. The corridor opens onto an indoor garden—serene, natural. The floor is leaf–green flagstone, the walls rose pink with white latticework. Natural palms, white wicker chairs and, overhead, a translucent dome create an environment as restorative as any country café in France. Upstairs are two cosy rooms enriched with Florentine oils, fireplaces, tapestries, chandeliers and candlelight.

Haute cuisine is at home here, as are proud but simple desserts. Hot Apple Charlotte is a rich fruity delight for all occasions, as is the Apple Cream Pie. As a special treat for family and friends, serve them the Orange Cream Tart. *Bon appetit!*

Orange Cream Tart

Preheat oven to 375°F.
9" - 10" removable tart pan.

Crust

1 1/2 cups flour
1/3 cup icing sugar — Combine.

6 oz butter — Add to above until dough forms ball. Pat into pan and bake until light brown, approximately 20-25 minutes. Cool on rack.

Pastry Cream

1 1/2 cups milk — Heat in saucepan, just until boiling. Turn heat to low.

5 egg yolks
1/3 cup sugar — Beat in clean bowl until blended.

1/3 cup flour — Add to yolks/sugar mixture and mix well. Add some of the hot milk to egg mixture, stir and pour back into hot milk. Beat on low heat until thick. Remove from heat.

2 tbsp butter
1/2 tbsp orange liqueur — Add to above and mix well. Pour onto cooled crust. Chill.

Topping

4-5 large oranges — Peel and remove skin then segment. Lay on top of chilled pastry cream.

1/4 cup apple jelly — Melt and brush over oranges.

This delicate pastry cream with sweet oranges is a heavenly dessert.

Apple Cream Pie

Preheat oven to 375°F.
9" - 10" removable pie pan.

Crust

1 tsp sugar 1 1/4 cups flour 3 oz butter 1 oz lard	Mix until crumbly.
3 tbsp cold water	Add until dough comes together. Pat into pan. Prebake 15-20 minutes until light brown. Cool on rack.
4 apples	Peel, core and slice thinly. Place into pan and bake 15 minutes.
1/2 cup sugar 1/2 cup cream 1 egg 1 tsp kirsch	Combine in bowl, and pour over apples. Continue baking 20 minutes until custard sets. Cool on rack, sprinkle with cinnamon.

Optional Topping

Before baking, prepare your favorite pastry crust and roll out a 9"–10" circle. Place over unbaked apples and custard, and bake until golden, approximately 20 minutes. Cool.

Apples and a hint of cream produce a wonderful version of apple pie.

Hot Apple Charlotte

Preheat oven to 400°F.
Butter a 6 cup soufflé dish and
   line bottom with buttered parchment paper.

1 oz raisins 1 tbsp rum	Soak raisins in rum. Set aside.
2 lbs golden delicious apples (approx. 6 large)	Peel, core and cut each apple into eighths.
4 tbsp sugar	Add to apples.
2 tbsp butter	Sauté apples in butter for approximately 8 minutes. Take off heat.
3 tbsp apricot jam 1 1/2 tbsp honey zest of 1/2 orange	Add to above. Mix. Add drained raisins. Set mixture aside.
1/2 loaf of egg bread or brioche	Cut into 1/2" slices. Sauté in melted butter until slightly brown and completely line bottom and sides of soufflé dish with bread. Cut bread to fit well. Pour apple mixture into dish. Top with remaining slices of browned bread. Cover with foil. Bake in water-bath for 40 minutes. Let stand 15 minutes before unmolding. Serve with Crème Anglaise. (see page 16.)

This buttery bread and hot apple combination is a rich fruity delight.

THE FOUR SEASONS 99 East 52 Street New York 10022

Outstanding is the most common superlative used to describe this quintessential New York restaurant, and for excellent reasons. It is here that diners, for thirty years, have experienced the epitome of western culture, sophistication, and *joie de vivre*.

As the name implies, The Four Seasons alters and evolves as each season passes. Four times a year new flowers and shrubs are planted, and the colors of the decor change to match leaves or sprouting grass, creating a vibrant environment of renewal.

There are two distinct and spacious dining areas. The Bar Room, bastion of publishing giants, is found at the top of a grand staircase. Modeled in French walnut paneling with pale linen-covered tables surrounded by blue banquettes and steel-framed chairs, this room reflects the essence of restraint. Tiny brass and copper chains looped across tall, tinted windows, add to a feeling of chic security. For dining on the lower level, the ever-popular Pool Room is reached through a long corridor. Tables, well-spaced for privacy, cluster around an elegant rectangular white marble pool which is cornered by tropical rubber trees. The movement of the water along with the gentle ripple of copper, brass and aluminum shutters makes the air electric.

The eclectic menu, too, changes seasonally as does the Spa Cuisine or low calorie menu. Dishes delight the eye and dazzle the palate. Desserts like Chocolate Velvet Cake are dense, moist and lush. The Four Seasons has shared its truly original Four Seasons Fancy Cake recipe too, a blissful marriage of Bavarian cream and orange chiffon.

Chocolate Velvet Cake

Preheat oven to 350°F.
Line a 10" x 15" jelly roll pan with
    buttered and floured parchment paper
6 cup mold dish.

Sponge

6 eggs $^3/_4$ cup sugar }	Beat until light and thick.
$^3/_4$ cup flour	Fold into above and pour into pan. Bake approximately 15 minutes until tester comes out clean. Cool on rack.

Chocolate Filling

2 egg yolks $^1/_2$ tbsp instant coffee 2 tbsp Kirsch (or fruit liqueur) 2 tbsp rum 2 tbsp chocolate or coffee liqueur 3 tbsp softened almond paste }	Beat until smooth.
3 tbsp melted butter	Add and beat until smooth.
12 oz melted semi-sweet chocolate	Add to above and beat well. Set aside.
2 egg whites	In clean bowl, beat until soft peaks form.
2 tbsp icing sugar	Add and beat until stiff. Set aside.
1 cup whipping cream	Beat in clean bowl until stiff. Fold whipped cream and egg whites into above chocolate mixture. Set aside.

Chocolate Velvet Cake
(continued)

Assembly

Take 6 cup mold dish and line bottom and sides with sponge cake. (Cut with knife to fit). Leave a piece for the top. Pour filling into sponge-lined mold, top with sponge cake, then refrigerate at least 1 $1/2$ to 2 hours. Loosen sides with knife and invert onto serving dish. Frost with icing. Sift icing sugar over top.

Chocolate Icing

6 oz semi-sweet chocolate	Melt and cool slightly.
$1/3$ cup whipping cream	Slowly add to above and mix well until smooth and thick.

A spectacular-looking dessert. The liqueur chocolate filling is dense, lush and simply outstanding.

Four Seasons Fancy Cake

Bavarian Cream – Part I

1 $^1/_2$ tbsp gelatin } $^1/_2$ cup milk }	Sprinkle over milk to soften. Set aside.
1 $^1/_4$ cups milk	Heat in top of double boiler.
3 egg yolks } $^1/_4$ cup sugar }	In separate bowl beat until blended. Add milk/gelatin mixture. Add heated milk, stir and place back on stove in the double boiler. Stir constantly until mixture coats a spoon, approximately 15 minutes. Remove from heat.
2 tbsp rum	Add, refrigerate approximately $^1/_2$ hour, or chill quickly by placing pot over bowl of ice water stirring occasionally. Meanwhile, make chiffon layer.

Preheat oven to 350°F.
Butter and flour 9"–10" springform.

Orange Chiffon Layer

1 cup cake flour } $^3/_4$ cup sugar } 1 $^1/_2$ tsp baking powder } $^1/_2$ tsp salt }	Sift into large bowl.
$^1/_4$ cup oil } 2 egg yolks } 6 tbsp orange juice } 1 $^1/_2$ tbsp finely grated orange peel }	Add to above and beat until smooth. Set aside.
4 egg whites	In clean bowl beat until stiff. Fold into above flour/orange juice mixture. Pour into pan and bake approx. 20-25 minutes or until tester comes out clean. Cool on rack.

Four Seasons Fancy Cake
(continued)

Bavarian Cream – Part II

3 egg whites	Beat until foamy.
$1/2$ cup sugar	Add and beat until stiff. Set aside.
1 cup heavy cream	In clean bowl, beat until stiff. Set $1/2$ aside for later use. Fold whites and $1/2$ of cream into above chilled Bavarian mixture.

Assembly of Cake

Spread reserved $1/2$ cup of whipped cream over chiffon cake. Pour Bavarian Cream over top, smooth and refrigerate.

Topping

8 oz softened almond paste } $1/4$ cup cocoa	Beat until combined. Knead until smooth. Roll out thin until diameter of springform pan. Place layer on top of Bavarian Cream. Sprinkle with icing sugar. Chill.

The combination of Bavarian Cream, orange chiffon and chocolate marzipan topping is well worth the effort.

The Silver Palate

It's just possible that the tiniest gourmet food shop in the world is tucked away in Manhattan. At The Silver Palate, windows are cheerfully cluttered with greenery and innumerable edible delights. And once through the door and into a room reminiscent of a large closet—no more than six customers will fit comfortably at once—wall-to-wall delicacies cram every available inch of space.

Sheila Lukins and Julee Rosso opened the Silver Palate at a time when very few women were in the food business. Both are passionate about fresh, in-season ingredients. Their shop is a haven for food lovers, offering some of the best take-out and catering of gourmet in the city.

Baked goods are fresh and delicious. Prepared morsels exquisitely fill glass display cases, and shelves abound with exotic and unusual eatables. Shoppers find a dazzling array of The Silver Palate's own bottled sauces, relishes, nut oils and herb vinegars. This miniature shop creates entrées daily, always from quality seasonal ingredients, and spiced and herbed to a lively flavor. The staff even prepare picnic hampers, items coordinated by taste.

Recipes gleaned from friends and colleagues have produced super desserts, like the perpetually popular Chocolate Mousse Cake. And this one is exceptional. Another chocolate delight is the Chocolate Chip Crumb Cake, easy to make and quick to disappear. Almond aficionados will find the creamy Almond Cheesecake exquisite.

Chocolate Chip Crumb Cake

Preheat oven to 325°F.
Butter and flour small bundt pan.

Topping

2 1/2 oz butter 1/2 cup sugar	Beat until smooth.
1 egg yolk 3/4 tbsp cinnamon	Add to above and beat until smooth.
1 cup flour	Fold into above until crumbly. Set aside.

Cake

6 oz butter 6 oz cream cheese	Cream until smooth.
3/4 cup sugar	Beat into above until well blended.
3 eggs	Add one at a time until blended.
1 cup flour 1 tsp baking powder 1 cup chocolate chips	Fold into above just until combined. Pour half into pan and sprinkle with half the topping. Pour remainder over top and finish with topping. Bake for approximately 35-45 minutes or until tester comes out clean. Cool on rack. Invert, and re-invert so that crumbs are on top. Sift icing sugar over top.

A truly buttery chocolate coffee cake.

Chocolate Mousse Layer Cake

Preheat oven to 350°F.
Line two 8"–9" pans with buttered and floured parchment paper.

Cake

1 cup boiling water $^{1}/_{2}$ cup cocoa	Mix in large bowl until cocoa dissolves.
4 oz butter 1 cup sugar	In separate bowl, cream until smooth.
2 eggs	Add to butter mixture and beat until smooth. Fold into cocoa mixture. Whisk well.
1 $^{1}/_{8}$ cup flour $^{3}/_{4}$ tsp baking soda $^{1}/_{4}$ tsp baking powder	Fold into above. Pour into cake pans and bake for approximately 20-25 minutes or until tester comes out clean. Set on rack to cool.

Mousse

8 oz semi-sweet chocolate	Melt and stir until smooth.
4 egg yolks $^{1}/_{4}$ cup Grand Marnier	Beat into chocolate until combined.
4 egg whites	Beat in clean bowl until stiff. Set aside.
1 cup heavy cream	Beat in clean bowl until stiff. Alternately fold whites and cream into chocolate mixture. Chill until of spreading consistency, approximately 30–40 minutes.

Chocolate Mousse Layer Cake
(continued)

Ganache

12 oz semi-sweet chocolate or 2 cups semi-sweet chocolate chips	Melt and stir until smooth.
1 cup heavy cream	Stir into chocolate until smooth and thick. Slightly reheat in microwave if consistency gets too thick to glaze.

Assembly

Invert cakes. Cut each cake into two layers. Place one layer on dish and spread some mousse over top. Repeat with other three layers. Ice sides and top of cake with thin layer of mousse. Chill. When mousse feels firm, ice with ganache and decorate with icing sugar or chocolate shavings.

A chocolate lover's paradise.

Sour Cream Almond Cheesecake

Preheat oven to 325°F.
8" buttered springform pan.

Crust

2 tbsp chopped almonds
1 cup graham cracker crumbs
2 tbsp sugar
4 tbsp butter
} Blend, and pat into bottom of pan. Refrigerate.

Filling

1 1/2 cups sliced blanched almonds — Toast on cookie sheet, or on top of stove until golden. Cool and grind in processor until fine. Set aside.

1 1/4 lb cream cheese
3/4 cup sugar
} Beat until smooth.

2 medium eggs — Add to above one at a time, and beat until smooth.

1/2 cup sour cream
1 1/2 tbsp vanilla
1/2 cup heavy cream
} Fold into above. Add toasted nuts and blend until well combined. Pour into crust and bake for approximately 60–70 minutes or until tester comes out clean.

Cool cake on rack and refrigerate until chilled. Decorate with sliced almonds and icing sugar.

This is an almond lover's delight.

WINDOWS ON THE WORLD

The 107th floor of the World Trade Center offers an almost extraterrestrial view of New York City. Windows On The World arrived two decades ago seemingly to fill secret longings—a space-like perspective of earth and a decent meal at a reasonable price.

Both out-of-towners and locals flock to this clever eatery for an above-it-all but breath-taking daytime glimpse of Manhattan's hustle and bustle. After dark the phenomenal panorama resembles the jewel-like glitter of a galaxy. This is undoubtedly the best view of one of the most exciting cities in the world.

With such spectacular horizons as the focus of attention, it's refreshing that the cuisine is not mundane. Windows On The World is so popular that reservations for dining close to the stars must be secured well in advance. There's also a dress code—no jeans—for what feels like a visit to a star ship.

Arrival itself is an experience. Diners are whisked up in ninety seconds, disembarking at a hall of mirrors. This corridor leads to the main room where the decor is a study of terran browns, neutral tones designed to call attention to the main attraction—viewing from terraced seating through three stories of glass. The crew of this restaurant serves up everything from familiar, basic, earth-bound meals to more complex creations.

Out-of-this-galaxy delectables abound, particularly the nutty Frozen Nougat Terrine, a dreamy Amaretto Cheesecake and Windows, famous Chocolate Sabayon Cake, a sponge cake laced with chocolate that can satisfy every mortal's sweet tooth.

Chocolate Sabayon Cake

Preheat oven to 350°F.
Line a 9" springform pan with buttered and floured parchment paper.

Chocolate Filling

5 egg yolks 4 tbsp sugar $1/3$ cup sherry or liqueur of choice	Heat in top of double boiler, whipping constantly, approximately 5-8 minutes, just until thick. Set aside.
4 oz semi-sweet chocolate	Melt. Set aside.
$1/2$ tbsp gelatin (Dissolve according to package)	Beat chocolate and dissolved gelatin into above egg mixture until combined.
1 $1/3$ cups whipping cream 2 tbsp icing sugar	Whip in clean bowl until stiff. Fold into above chocolate/egg mixture. Place in refrigerator approximately 1 hour until of spreading consistency. Meanwhile make cake.

Cake

4 eggs $3/4$ cup sugar	Beat until pale, approximately 5 minutes.
$1/3$ cup flour 2 tsp cornstarch 4 tbsp cocoa	Sift and fold into above. Pour into pan. Bake for approximately 25 minutes or until tester comes out dry. Cool on rack.

Assembly

Slice cake in half. Carefully remove top layer. Leave bottom half in pan and spread $1/3$ of filling over top of cake. Place second layer over top and repeat with $1/3$ of filling. Chill remaining filling and cake for 30 minutes. Unmold and frost sides with remaining filling. Decorate with icing sugar or chocolate shavings. Refrigerate.

A light sponge cake with an airy chocolate filling.

Frozen Nougat Terrine

4 cup decorative mold.   Recipe may be doubled.

2 eggs (medium)
2 egg yolks (medium)
$^1/_3$ cup sugar

Whip with beaters until white, approximately 5 minutes. Set aside.

Nougat (Hazelnut paste)

1 $^1/_2$ cups hazelnuts or almonds
1 $^1/_4$ cups icing sugar
$^1/_2$ tsp almond extract
1 egg white

Grind until creamy. Set aside. Measure 2 oz of paste and whip into above egg/sugar mixture. Refrigerate remainder for future use.

1 cup whipping cream

Whip until firm. Fold into above mixture and pour into mold. Freeze for approximately 3 hours. Invert by setting mold in hot water for 30 seconds and quickly inverting onto serving dish. Serve with strawberry sauce.

Strawberry Sauce

1 cup strawberries
Grand Marnier or
other liqueur to taste.

Purée until smooth.

Tastes like a rich nutty ice cream.

Amaretto Cream Cheesecake

Preheat oven to 325°F.
8" springform pan.

Crust

1 cup graham cracker crumbs 3 tbsp soft butter $^1/_2$ tbsp almonds	Grind until crumbs loosely hold together. Pat onto bottom of pan. Refrigerate while making filling.

Filling

1 $^1/_2$ lbs cream cheese (three 8 oz packages)	Beat until smooth.
$^1/_2$ cup sugar	Add and continue beating until smooth.
3 eggs	Add one at a time until blended.
$^1/_3$ cup sour cream	Add and blend.
$^2/_3$ heavy cream $^1/_2$ cup amaretto liqueur	Add to above, blend well and pour into pan. Bake for approximately 1 hour or until 1" in center appears a little loose. Cool on rack. Refrigerate until chilled. Decorate with toasted sliced almonds, or with sliced fresh fruit.

Almond liqueur gives this creamy cheesecake
a new, subtle flavor.

The Plaza

When The Plaza opened in 1907, it was billed as the most luxurious hotel in the world. Now, creeping up on ninety years, this grand dame, still the essence of tradition and sophistication, remains serenely unchanged. While the building itself, a marvel of French Renaissance architecture, has, naturally, undergone some alterations through the years, what seems remarkable is that The Plaza today looks very much as it always has.

Of the many dining rooms at The Plaza Hotel, The Palm Court is probably the most popular. As with the rest of the hotel, no corners are cut to maintain its elegance. To verify the sense that here time stands still, a large portrait of Eloise, the charming, precocious, beloved star of children's books who has for decades been synonymous with The Plaza, impishly grins approval at diners entering The Palm Court. The dining area itself is resplendent, in the Viennese style. Brown marble table-tops with a single cut flower on each, elaborate glass and crystal lighting, arched mirrored doors, sedate furnishings, classical statuary atop gold-leafed pillars—all in good taste and surrounded by thick sprays of the dark, green-potted palms for which this room was named.

The Palm Court is a wonderful place for afternoon tea. While drinking from fragile china cups and consuming open-faced sandwiches and rich pastries reminiscent of Viennese coffeehouse fare, the mood is further enhanced by a piano and violin duet performing euphonious waltz pieces.

Pastry chef Eric Bedoucha, in charge of all desserts at The Plaza, recommends the Raspberry Truffle Cake, as light and airy as the music played in The Palm Court. On the other hand, the Apricot Walnut Cake has a solid nutty goodness that taste buds applaud. Try the Plum Tart for an unusual and delightful fruity treat. And surely only the Plaza Hotel could offer Chocolate Lady Fingers, perhaps the classiest dessert ever created.

Raspberry Truffle Cake
(Lady Mogador)

Preheat oven to 350°F.
8" springform pan buttered and floured.

Chocolate Biscuit

4 egg yolks $^1/_3$ cup sugar	Beat until a light lemon color.
4 egg whites $^1/_3$ cup sugar	In clean bowl, beat until stiff. Carefully fold into above yolk mixture.
$^1/_4$ cup flour 2 tbsp cocoa $^1/_2$ tbsp cornstarch	Sift and gently fold into above egg mixture.
2 oz melted butter	Add to above and mix gently. Pour into pan and bake approximately 20-25 minutes or until tester comes out clean. Cool on rack.

Truffle Mixture

8 oz semi-sweet chocolate	Melt and stir until smooth.
1 $^1/_2$ cups whipping cream $^1/_4$ cup sugar	In clean bowl beat until stiff. Gently fold into chocolate. Set aside.
$^1/_2$ cup raspberries $^1/_4$ cup raspberry jam 2 tbsp fruit liqueur (preferably raspberry or kirsch)	Set aside.

Assembly

Release side of springform and carefully slice cake in half. Remove upper half. Replace side part of pan to hold. Brush bottom layer of cake with liqueur and then jam. Place raspberries over top. Pour truffle mixture over top of raspberries. Crumble other cake layer over truffle. Sprinkle with icing sugar.

Raspberries and chocolate provide a sweet and tangy combination.

Apricot Walnut Cake

Preheat oven to 350°F.
Butter and flour 10" springform pan.

8 egg yolks 2/3 cup sugar	Beat until light and thick.
8 egg whites 3/4 cup sugar	In clean bowl, beat until stiff. Gently fold into above.
2/3 cup cake flour 1 cup finely ground walnuts 1 tsp cornstarch	Sift together and gently fold into above yolks/whites mixture.
4 oz melted butter	Fold into above and pour into pan. Bake approximately 35-40 minutes or until tester comes out clean. Cool on rack. Unmold cake and carefully slice into 3 equal layers. Remove top 2 layers of cake with the aid of spatulas.
1/4 cup fruit liqueur	Brush 1/3 of liqueur over bottom layer.
1/2 cup apricot jam	Warm jam so it becomes easier to spread. Spread 1/3 over liqueur. Repeat with other 2 layers. Top cake layer with jam, and spread over sides as well.
1/4 cup finely ground walnuts	Sprinkle over cake. Serve with Crème Anglaise, if desired. (see page 16).

Apricot is the best jam to use, but substitute, if you like, with your favorite.

Chocolate Lady Fingers

Preheat oven to 375°F.
Butter a cookie sheet and line
   with buttered parchment paper.

Makes approximately 20 cookies.

3 egg whites	Beat until foamy.
4 tbsp sugar	Add and beat until stiff. Set aside.
3 egg yolks	Beat until mixed.
1 $1/4$ cups icing sugar	Add to yolks and continue beating until thick. Fold yolk mixture into whites.
$1/2$ cup pastry flour 2 $1/2$ tbsp cocoa	Sift and fold into above. Mix until well combined. Pipe lady fingers onto sheet with decorating tube (approx. 4" long, and 1" wide). Bake for approximately 10 minutes, just until browned. Cool.

*Delicate cookies that can stand alone or be eaten
with custard or mousse.*

Plum Tart

Preheat oven to 350°F.

9" - 10" flan pan.

Crust

1 1/2 cups flour ⎫ 1/3 cup icing sugar ⎬ 6 oz butter ⎭	Combine until dough comes together and forms a ball. Pat into pan. Prebake 20-25 minutes or until crust is light brown. Set aside.
Pastry cream - see page 68	Prepare recipe for cream and pour over crust.
6 - 8 large plums	Peel, slice each plum into thin wedges and place over top of pastry cream. Sprinkle with sugar. Bake approximately 20 minutes, just until fruit is tender. Cool on rack.
2 tbsp apple or red currant jelly	Warm and brush over cake. Serve jelly warm with Crème Anglaise, if desired (see page 16).

This delicate fruit tart can also be made with
fresh nectarines or apricots.

La Côte Basque

For gourmets, La Côte Basque on New York's East Side epitomizes cuisine magnifique with the added bonus of a smart, lively and romantic setting.

Diners select from a wide array of classic French dishes, served with unusual flair in a convivial environment. Much of the carving, flambéing, sautéing and saucing occurs at tableside under the capable hands of an affable chef. The decor in this generous space creates much of the cheerfulness through images of the sunny feel of France's charming Côte Basque. Cherry-red leather banquettes, ivory walls, near-black beams and timbers and a 'view' of the town of St. Jean de Luz through *trompe l'oeil* windows blend nicely with the blues, tans and greens of Bernard Lamotte's murals of seascapes and waterfront cafés. The menu is extensive. Specialties include pepper steak, Dover sole and quail prepared with humor and finesse.

Dozens of astonishing desserts highlight the *nouvelle patisserie* offerings. Mixes or sugaring the imported fruits is taboo at La Côte Basque. Desserts utilize Jamaican rum pastes, French pears, imported fruit purées and European chocolate, but focus on fresh cream, ripe berries and butter, butter, butter. Almond Dacquoise is just one: a rich sweet buttercream is highlighted. Chocolate Meringue Mousse blends crusty with creamy textures for an unusual taste treat, astonishingly rich yet unbelievably light.

Amaretto Cream Cheesecake, page 42 ▷

Almond Dacquoise

Preheat oven to 300°F.
3 large cookie sheets lined with buttered and floured parchment paper.
Draw 3 8" circles onto paper.

10 egg whites	Beat until half their volume.
3 tbsp sugar	Add, beating until stiff.
1 1/4 cups ground toasted almonds 3/4 cup sugar }	Combine in clean bowl.
2 cups icing sugar 1 tbsp cornstarch }	Sift into almond mixture, then fold carefully into egg whites. Pipe 3 filled-in circles onto parchment paper using a spoon or pastry bag. With remainder of meringue, pipe long cylinder shapes beside each circle (to be used for decoration). Bake for 1 1/4 –1 1/2 hours, or until meringue is crisp and golden. Cool on rack.

Buttercream

2/3 cup sugar 1/2 cup corn syrup }	Stir over medium heat until mixture boils. Remove from heat.
4 egg yolks	In clean bowl, whip until thick and pale. Beat in sugar mixture until cool, approximately 3-5 minutes.
1 2/3 cups butter	Beat into above, piece by piece.
1/4 cup amaretto	Mix into above. Refrigerate until consistency is right for icing.

Assembly
    Use half of the buttercream to frost each meringue layer, stack layers, then, with the other half of the buttercream, ice tops and sides with remaining half of buttercream. Crush piped cylinder pieces of meringue and decorate cake on top and sides with these pieces.

The texture of crunchy meringue and smooth buttercream is wonderful.

 Strawberry Cream Dacquoise (Boccone Dolce) page 52

Chocolate Meringue Mousse

6-8 individual dishes.

12 oz semi-sweet chocolate ⎫ 6 oz butter ⎰	Melt and stir until smooth.
4 egg yolks	Add to above and mix until smooth. Set aside.
6 egg whites	In clean bowl beat until foamy.
1/3 cup sugar	Add and beat until stiff. Fold into chocolate mixture. Spoon into dishes and refrigerate. Sprinkle with icing sugar and cocoa powder.

The thickest and darkest mousse ever!

SARDI'S

Since 1921, Sardi's has been synonymous with theater. Top Broadway actors, playwrights, producers and directors head for Sardi's on opening nights and regularly before and after curtain. Audiences, too, crowd into this medium-sized bar/restaurant hoping to catch a glimpse of the stars.

Step inside to the coat checkroom, and from there make an entrance into the tiny bar and white-linened dining area. But up the stairs is the main attraction. This principal bar, set in almost an attic, is dimly lit with a low ceiling—automatic intimacy. Every inch of wall space features the legendary, colored caricatures that are part of the charm and mystique. A few tables with gingham tablecloths exist, but standing at the bar is far more exciting. The crowd is always lively and boisterous. Watching the cheek-kissing is built-in entertainment, and customers are expected to rub shoulders with celebs.

Food in this theatrical ambience leans towards the dramatic. Continental cuisine is served with a flair by clippy, city-smart waiters. When it comes to desserts, the Strawberry Cream Dacquoise is a long-running hit. For simpler tastes, try Date Rice Pudding, an example of why New York's theater district and Sardi's are special.

Strawberry Cream Dacquoise
(Boccone Dolce)

Preheat oven to 275°F.
Butter 3 cookie sheets and line
    with buttered and floured parchment paper.
Draw three 8" circles on paper.

Meringue Layers

1 cup egg whites (approx. 6 or 7 large) 1/4 tsp cream of tartar }	Beat until stiff.
2 cups sugar	Add gradually to eggs and beat until glossy. Spread meringue evenly over circles, approximately 1/2 inch thick, and bake for 1 1/2 to 2 hours, or until meringue is pale gold. Rotate position in oven if meringues are getting too brown. Remove from oven, cool and carefully remove parchment paper.

Filling

4 oz semi-sweet chocolate 2 tbsp water }	Melt, stir and set aside.
3 cups whipping cream	Whip until stiff.
1/3 cup icing sugar	Add to cream and beat until very stiff. Set aside.
1 pint fresh strawberries	Slice and set aside.

Assembly

    Place one meringue layer on serving plate, and carefully spread with a thin covering of melted chocolate. Warm chocolate again slightly if too thick. Spread a layer about 3/4" thick of whipped cream on top and place a layer of strawberries over cream. Repeat with other two meringue layers. Frost tops and sides of baked meringue with remainder of whipped cream. Decorate with remaining strawberries, or drizzle any remaining chocolate over whipped cream. Refrigerate 2 hours before serving.

Meringue, strawberries, cream and chocolate—what a Combo!

Date Rice Pudding

Preheat oven to 350°F.
6 cup oven casserole dish.

2 1/2 cups milk 1/4 cup rice (uncooked)	Bring to boil. Simmer 50 minutes, stirring occasionally.
1 egg 1/3 cup sugar 1/2 tsp salt 1/4 tsp vanilla	Beat together in bowl. Add hot rice and milk to egg mixture. Stir well.
1 cup cream	Add to above.
1/2 cup raisins 1/2 cup chopped dates	Place in bottom of dish. Pour mixture over fruit. Stir. Sprinkle with cinnamon and sugar. Bake in water bath for 30 minutes. Cool on rack, then chill.

Dates give this old-time favorite a real twist.

CARNEGIE
DELICATESSEN & RESTAURANT

Deli food has universal appeal. There are at least three factors that contribute to the almost mythical reputation of the Carnegie Delicatessen. Located just off the theater district, crowds can follow the tangy scents to this hallowed landmark. And the fact that this restaurant is open just short of twenty-four hours is a godsend for both New Yorkers and tourists alike. But the overwhelming draw is an astonishingly diverse menu.

For anyone unfamiliar with this continuously popular New York institution, the Carnegie Deli was the set for Woody Allen's film, *Broadway Danny Rose*. Here regulars and newcomers alike find the epitome of casual food, served by cheerful, wisecracking waiters in a brightly lit, near raucous environment. Customers are welcomed however they're dressed—tuxedoed or blue-jeaned.

Generous servings of homemade soups, juicy burgers, fish dishes, chicken, a wide selection of sandwiches including the thickest pastrami on rye available anywhere—the list goes on and on.

A veritable cornucopia of tasty, familiar and scrumptious desserts beckons. Outrageous helpings of Carnegie's Famous Cheesecake can be served plain or topped with fruits—strawberry, blueberry, cherry or pineapple are the usual. For an excellent way to greet the morning, try Chocolate Cinnamon Crescents. And the Grand Marnier Chocolate Truffle Torte is so rich it must be experienced to be believed.

Carnegie's Famous Cheesecake

Preheat oven to 400°F.
Butter a 9" springform pan.

Crust (sugar dough)

4 oz sugar 6 oz butter	Cream until well combined.
1 1/2 cups flour 1 tbsp lemon zest 1 tsp vanilla	Add until crumbly and work until mixture then comes together. Pat into bottom and sides of pan and prebake approximately 15-20 minutes until light brown. Cool on rack.

Cheese Filling

2 lb cream cheese (4 - 8 oz packages) 1 cup sugar	Cream until smooth.
2 eggs 1 tbsp lemon juice 1/2 tbsp vanilla 2 tbsp cornstarch	Add and mix until well blended.
1 cup sour cream	Fold into above and pour into prebaked pan. Bake for approx. 45-50 minutes or just until center is a little loose. If cakes begins to brown, cover with foil. Leave in oven with door open and temperature off until cool. Chill. Top with icing sugar or fresh berries.

This truly represents New York style cheesecake.

Grand Marnier Chocolate Truffle Torte

Preheat oven to 350°F.
Line a 9" springform pan and one 9" round cake pan
    with buttered and floured parchment paper.

Sugar Dough

3 oz butter 6 tbsp sugar	Cream until smooth.
1/2 egg	Add until combined.
1 1/3 cup flour 1 1/2 tbsp cocoa	Sift and fold into above.
1 tbsp water	Add and combine until dough comes together. Place into bottom of springform and refrigerate while making torte.

Torte

3 1/2 oz semi-sweet chocolate	Melt and stir until smooth. Set aside.
2 oz butter 2 1/2 tbsp sugar	In separate bowl, cream until smooth. Add to chocolate and combine well.
2 egg yolks 3 whole eggs	Add to above until all incorporated.
2 tbsp flour	Fold into above.
2 egg whites 1 tbsp sugar	Beat in clean bowl until stiff. Fold into above. Pour into 9" round cake pan. Bake approximately 30-40 minutes or until tester comes out dry. Cool on rack. Now bake prepared sugar dough about 20-25 minutes until tester comes out dry. Cool on rack.

Grand Marnier Chocolate Truffle Torte
(continued)

Chocolate Truffle

2 cups whipping cream	Beat until stiff. Set aside.
7 oz semi-sweet chocolate	Melt and stir until smooth.
1 tbsp Grand Marnier	Add to chocolate until blended.
1 tsp gelatin	Dissolve according to package instructions until melted. Add to chocolate mixture until combined. Fold in whipped cream until combined.

Assembly

Pour 1/3 truffle mixture over cookie crust. Invert torte and slice into two layers. Carefully place one layer over chocolate truffle, cover with another 1/3 truffle mixture, top with second torte layer and ice top with remaining truffle mixture. Refrigerate for at least 2–3 hours. Decorate with icing sugar.

A richer truffle filling has never been created.

Chocolate Cinnamon Crescents
(Chocolate Rugelach)

Preheat oven to 375°F.   Makes 36 crescents
Butter and flour one large cookie sheet.

6 oz cream cheese 6 oz butter	Cream until smooth.
$1/4$ cup icing sugar $1/2$ tsp vanilla	Add until combined.
2 cups flour	Add until mixture combines and is no longer sticky. Add more flour if too sticky. Cut dough into 3 sections. On a floured board, roll out each section of dough in a circle to $1/8$" thickness.
2 tbsp melted butter	Brush with melted butter.
$2/3$ cup ground nuts $1/3$ cup raisins 2 tbsp cinnamon $1/3$ cup sugar $1/2$ cup chocolate chips	Sprinkle in this order over each of the 3 circles. Cut each circle into 12 wedges. Roll up from wide edge to narrow part. Place on cookie sheet and bake 20 minutes until golden brown.

Chocolate chips make these cookies outstanding.

RAINB◉W.

The Rainbow Room is perhaps the last of the formal supper clubs. Visiting this black-tie environment is like taking a step back in time to another, more glamorous, romantic era. Created decades ago as a second home where New York's elite could socialize, the Rainbow Room now caters to a diverse clientele, including a younger crowd that finds the ambience fascinating.

In a dramatic ballroom setting straight out of the 30s, diners chit-chat over cocktails, sample some very fine French and American cuisine and then dance to the music of a big band until the wee hours. In bygone years the likes of Mary Martin as well as Edgar Bergen and Charlie McCarthy performed here. This spacious room is located high up in the RCA Building in Rockefeller Plaza. The designer obviously had glamor in mind, which accounts for enormous chandeliers, elegant table settings, and lots of mirrors on the walls in which to catch a profusion of images.

Desserts, too, have an aura of gaiety and splendor about them. What could be more unusual than Praline Soufflé with Chocolate Sauce. And the Baked Alaska with Fruit Sauce will linger in your memory long after it's gone.

Frozen Praline Soufflé with Chocolate Sauce

5 individual serving cups or
  a 4-6 cup mold.

Praline

$1/2$ cup sugar ⎱ 2 $1/2$ tbsp water ⎰	Cook until sugar bubbles and thickens, approximately 5 minutes on medium-high heat. Do not let this turn brown.
$1/3$ cup chopped nuts (of your choice)	Add and stir until combined. Nuts become coated like candy. Cool on cookie sheet. Grind into small pieces in food processor. Set aside.
2 eggs ⎫ 1 egg yolk ⎬ $1/3$ cup sugar ⎭	Place in double boiler. Heat until sugar is absorbed. Whip at high-speed until thick and pale, approximately 5 minutes. Set aside.
$1/3$ cup almond paste	Soften paste by slightly warming it; then beat into above egg mixture.
2 cups whipping cream	Whip until soft peaks form. Fold into above almond/egg mixture. Add chopped praline until combined. Pour into molds. Turn out by setting molds into hot water for a few seconds. Serve with chocolate sauce. (see page 24).

Tastes better than ice cream.

Baked Alaska with Fruit Sauce

8" springform pan.

12 oz ready- bought sponge cake or follow recipe on page 30	Slice in 1/4" thick slices. Line bottom and sides of springform with sponge cake. Leave remainder of cake for top.
1 pint soft chocolate ice cream 1 pint soft raspberry or strawberry sorbet 1 pint soft vanilla ice cream	Layer ice cream in this order over sponge cake. Top with some of remaining sponge cake and freeze, approx. 1 1/2 hours. Meanwhile make sauce.

Fruit Sauce

1/4 cup water 1/3 cup sugar 1 tsp vanilla	Place in saucepan on high heat until mixture becomes syrupy, approx. 3-5 minutes. Remove from heat.
2 oz raspberries 2 oz blueberries 4 oz strawberries, sliced	Add to syrup. Cool.

Meringue

Preheat oven to 450°F

4 egg whites 1/4 cup sugar	In clean bowl, beat until stiff. Cover frozen cake completely with meringue.

Place cake in oven until lightly brown, approx. 5–10 minutes
Serve immediately with sauce.

A classic dessert made to impress.

FRENCH RESTAURANT

Spectacular is *le mot juste* for Le Cirque—a chic yet unpretentious neighborhood eatery where diners find the lightest haute cuisine available in New York in a high-charged ambience.

Monkey murals add a touch of circus whimsy to an otherwise grand and elegant decor. This frenetic kinetic establishment is always packed with high-powered international glitterati. Even the great chefs dine here, at what has been termed New York's best French restaurant, confirming that the food can be counted on to be superb. The kitchen is given to experimentation and regularly produces exciting, nearly stunning dishes. An impressively large menu boasts forty-four entrées and twelve specials; diners need never repeat a meal.

Le Cirque is one of the few four-star restaurants in New York. Daniel Boulud, the chef, takes great pride in Le Cirque, which has been rated as the number one restaurant in the U.S.A. by Gault Millau, 1989, and the fourth best restaurant in the world by Robin Leach of *Lifestyles of the Rich and Famous.*

Desserts are legendary and Le Cirque provides one of the finest selections in the city. Crème Brulée—custard sprinkled with sugar and passed beneath a broiler until browned—is the specialty and utterly delicious. Try the Crisp Millefeuille with Fresh Fruit from the restaurant with a reputation for its continual ability to captivate patrons.

Crisp Millefeuille With Fresh Fruit

Preheat oven to 375°F.   4 servings
Butter and flour one cookie sheet.

Puff Pastry

Use 12 oz of frozen prepared pastry	Roll pastry out to $1/8$" thickness. Keep it as square as possible, approx. 10" x 14". Cut out 12 circles, each approx. 3" in diameter. Place on cookie sheet, pierce dough with a fork and place an empty baking pan over dough to flatten. Bake approx. 15 minutes, remove top pan, then bake approx. 10 more minutes, or just until golden. Cool.
2 pints strawberries } 2 pints raspberries }	Combine $1/2$ pint of each berry and purée for sauce. Leave the rest of berries for assembly.
$1/2$ cup water } 2 tbsp sugar } $1/2$ lemon squeeze }	Add to above purée and mix well. Set aside.
1 cup whipping cream } 4 tbsp icing sugar }	Beat until soft peaks are formed. Set aside.

Assembly

3 circles per serving (one stacked on top of one another). On top of one circle place some whipped cream. Layer with sliced strawberries. Place another circle on plate, add whipped cream and then whole raspberries. Add top circle. Repeat with remainder of circles. Sprinkle icing sugar over top and serve with reserved strawberry/ raspberry sauce.

Light puff pastry and fruit is a French classic.

Crème Brûlée

Preheat oven to 325°F.
5-6 individual oven dishes.

2 cups heavy cream ⎫
1 tbsp vanilla ⎭   Heat in saucepan just until warm.

5 tbsp sugar ⎫
4 egg yolks ⎭   Mix in separate bowl. Pour into above cream mixture and mix well. Pour into oven dishes. Cook in a bain-marie (water bath) for approx. 40-50 minutes or until set. Let cool in refrigerator. Sprinkle brown sugar on top. Put under broiler until melted and brown. Serve immediately.

An old-time French favorite.

Strawberry and Kiwi Cream Tart, page 68 ▷

RESTAURANT

Dining at the classic French restaurant, Le Cygne, recalls more than the grace and beauty of the swan, the bird for which it is named. In this dazzling establishment, a sense of mystery, even a fairy-tale quality, lingers.

Located in an East Side brownstone, Le Cygne unfolds as an impeccable environment. Muted lighting glides over subdued pastel and grey walls, and a peaked ceiling and the subtlest impressionistic wildflower murals create a gentle postmodern room on the main floor. In contrast to such fragility, the Wine Room above utilizes dark wood beams along an arched ceiling, rough brick walls and clay tile floors to create a strong Medieval mood. Dining is intimate.

Fowl, game and fish are the specialties. As well, frogs' legs, duck, pigeon and rabbit are treated by the kitchen with the respect such exotic fare deserves. Sauces are never overdone. Spicing reflects country cooking.

For an ending worthy of praise, try Le Cygne's Chocolate Mousse Roulade, chocolate ensconced in chocolate. Or the Strawberry and Kiwi Cream Tart. For the ultimate in richness and freshness, the lighter-than-air Raspberry Mousse served with strawberry sauce can't be equalled.

Chocolate Mousse Roulade, page 66

Chocolate Mousse Roulade

Preheat oven to 425°F.
Butter a jelly roll pan and line with buttered, floured parchment paper.

Sponge Roll

5 egg yolks
7 tbsp sugar } Beat until pale, approximately 3 minutes.

2 tbsp cake flour
2 1/2 tbsp cocoa } Sift and fold into above.

5 egg whites
1 tbsp sugar } Beat in clean bowl just until stiff. Fold into above. Pour into pan and bake for 5-7 minutes or until tester comes out clean. Cool on rack. Sprinkle with cocoa, place tea towel over cake and invert onto large cookie sheet. Peel off paper carefully. Set aside.

Mousse

4 oz semi-sweet chocolate — Melt and stir until smooth.

1 cup whipping cream — Pour over chocolate and whip until smooth. Let rest in refrigerator if necessary until of spreading consistency. Spread over cake evenly, and roll up cake like a jelly roll. Chill.

Chocolate Ganache

4 oz semi-sweet chocolate — Melt and stir until smooth.

1/2 cup heavy cream — Pour over chocolate and whip until smooth. Refrigerate if necessary until thick enough to frost. Ice top and sides of cake. Decorate with icing sugar. Serve with Cointreau sauce (optional).

Cointreau Sauce

1 cup melted vanilla ice cream
2 tbsp orange liqueur } Blend and serve under slices of cake.

Chocolate, chocolate and more chocolate!

Raspberry Mousse with Strawberry Sauce

4 cup decorative mold
or 4 individual dishes.

1 cup raspberry purée (approx. 20 oz raspberries)	Place in large bowl.
1 tbsp gelatin dissolved according to package ⎫ 1/2 cup raspberry liqueur ⎭	Blend well and mix into above purée.
2 cups whipping cream ⎫ 6 tbsp sugar ⎭	In clean bowl, beat until firm. Fold into above. Pour into molds. Refrigerate until set— approximately 3-4 hours. Unmold by dipping mold into hot water for approximately 30 seconds. Invert. Decorate with raspberries.

Strawberry Sauce

1 cup strawberry purée ⎫ (approx. 20 oz strawberries) ⎬ 1/2 tsp lemon juice ⎭	Blend and pour some over mousse.

*Raspberries and strawberries together provide the ultimate
in richness and freshness.*

Strawberry and Kiwi Cream Tart

Preheat oven to 375°F.
10" flan pan.

Crust

1 1/2 cups flour 1/3 cup icing sugar	Combine.
6 oz butter	Add to above until dough comes together. Pat into pan and bake approx. 20-25 minutes until golden brown. Cool on rack. Make pastry cream.

Pastry Cream

1 1/2 cups milk	Heat in saucepan, just until boiling. Turn heat to low.
5 egg yolks 1/3 cup sugar	Beat in clean bowl until blended.
1/3 cup flour	Add to yolk/sugar mixture and mix well. Add some milk to egg mixture, stir and pour back into hot milk. Beat on low heat until thick, approx. 5 minutes.
2 tbsp butter 1/2 tbsp Kirsch or other fruit liqueur	Add to above and mix well. Cool. Spread thick, cool pastry cream over crust.
1/2 pint sliced strawberries 3 sliced kiwis	Decorate with sliced fruits.
3 tbsp jelly glaze	Brush with apple or strawberry glaze.

Various bright, fresh fruits make this a light and artistic-looking dessert.
Feel free to substitute sliced fruits of your choice.

La Réserve is the marvelous creation of Jean-Louis Missud. This French salute to *gastronomie* is a haven for culinary purists. Every aspect —decor, service and cuisine—has been finely tuned to perfection, never boring or disappointing.

This is a restful, flattering environment for relaxed but serious diners. Comfortable lime velvet armchairs accompany banquettes upholstered in two glistening shades of peach. Comfort is enhanced by plush carpeting, paneled walls and lit mirrored ceilings. Illumination also comes from chandeliers, snowy glass fixtures and candlelight sprinkled throughout the room. The china's apt and graceful design was created by Missud's artist daughter. But the most striking element of La Réserve's decor is the glorious murals depicting quail, grouse, egrets and other wildfowl in nature settings: woods, lakes, and the like.

Game, of course, is the natural food here. Renowned head chef, André Gaillard, leads a team of cooks towards excellence. Each dish is resplendent with savory surprises. A culinary pace is attained that dazzles most diners, the main reason reservations are difficult to obtain. Careful service is the norm with, for instance, soups ladled into the plate at table. This is one restaurant where customers can, with confidence, place themselves safely in the hands of waiters and not be disappointed.

Pick out the subtle flavors in the Hazelnut Buttercream Cake with Anise. The Tarte Tartin will be a hit even with the most discriminating guests.

Tarte Tartin

Preheat oven to 375°F.
8" - 9" skillet pan that can be placed in oven.

Pastry

    Use 10 oz of frozen puff pastry.   Set aside.

Apple Mixture

4 large apples	Peel, core and slice each apple into eight sections. Set aside.
3 oz soft butter 2/3 cup sugar }	Spread out in skillet. Begin to warm on medium heat and place cut apples over top. Two layers of apples will be necessary. Cook on medium heat for approximately 15 minutes, until you see some light caramel on the sides. Roll puff pastry to the size of skillet and place over apples. Freeze remainder for another use. Prick with a fork. Sprinkle with sugar and bake approximately 25–30 minutes, or until crust becomes golden. Cool on rack slightly, then place skillet in refrigerator for 1 1/2 hours. Just before serving, place pan over high heat on stove and heat for approximately 1 minute. Carefully invert cake onto large serving dish. Spill off extra liquid. Serve immediately.

*A classic French favorite of an upside-down apple tart
that is simple to prepare.*

Hazelnut Buttercream Cake with Anise

Preheat oven to 350°F.
Line a 10" x 12" jelly roll pan with buttered and floured parchment paper.

Cake

2 tsp licorice liqueur 6 eggs 3/4 cup sugar }	Beat until light and thick.
3/4 cup flour	Fold into above gently until combined. Pour into pan. Bake approximately 10-15 minutes or until tester comes out clean. Cool on rack.

Buttercream

4 egg yolks	Beat until thick. Set aside.
2/3 cup sugar 2 tbsp water }	Cook until mixture begins to bubble, approx. 2 minutes; do not let brown. Quickly remove from stove and pour into yolks, beating all the time.
1 1/4 cups soft butter cut in pieces.	Add piece by piece, beating constantly.
1/4 cup licorice liqueur	Add and continue beating until mixture is smooth. Set aside.
1 cup chopped and toasted hazelnuts	Add to above buttercream mixture, blend and set aside.
3 oz melted chocolate	Set aside.

Assembly

Slice cake into 3 equal layers. Brush 2 layers with melted chocolate. Let set for 5-10 minutes. Place one layer with chocolate on serving plate and 1/3 buttercream on top. Repeat with both remaining cake layers. Ice sides and top with remaining buttercream (leaving cake with no chocolate for the top layer). Garnish with toasted coconut, if desired. Serve at room temperature.

Licorice flavor and hazelnuts together with a smooth buttercream is truly unique.

GOTHAM
Bar and Grill

Take 5,000 square feet of raw warehouse space with an out-of-sight
ceiling, plunk it down in the heart of Soho, and you've got either an
artists' cooperative, a three-ringed circus or a fabulously fashionable
eatery.

Gotham Bar & Grill has won the Restaurant and Hotel Design award
because what has been done with this cavernous environment is nothing
short of a miracle. Exciting, sophisticated, a tribute to postmodernism,
this is a place to make an entrance. Chintz-covered banquettes, fixtures
wrapped in aqua-trimmed parachute cloth, glass and mirrors forever—
all create a vital, contemporary eatery in the world's most cosmopolitan
city.

The number of diners passing through Gotham Bar & Grill each week
is phenomenal. Surprisingly, even though vast quantities are prepared,
quality is consistently high. An unusual range of successful dishes comes
out of a kitchen that rivals Grand Central Station. Squab, grilled tuna,
squid, lobster, goat cheese ravioli, even uncommon vegetables like Swiss
chard put in an appearance.

Classic desserts live side by side with zesty new creations at the
Gotham Bar & Grill. Try the creamy Crème Brûlée or the refreshing
Five Fruit and Berry Compote. And for something completely different,
serve Vanilla Poached Pears with Figs and Apricots, a mixture of fresh
and dried fruits in sweet syrup. Each of these desserts is easy to create, a
light and lively ending for any meal.

Vanilla Poached Pears
with Figs and Apricots

6 individual plates.   Serves 6

2 cups white wine 2 cups water 1 1/4 cups sugar pinch of ground cloves 1 tbsp vanilla 1 orange peeled and sliced 1 lemon squeezed	Combine in large saucepan.
3 large pears (preferably Bosc)	Peel, core, slice in half and add to above. Bring liquid to simmer and poach until pears are tender, approx. 20 minutes. Remove pears and store in 1/2 of cooking liquid. Chill. Reserve other half of liquid. Do not strain.
8 dried figs 16 dried apricots	Poach in remaining unstrained syrup until tender, approx. 20 minutes. Remove from heat.
4 tbsp rum	Add to fig mixture. Chill.

Serve 1/2 pear to each person with the chilled apricots and figs
and a little syrup.

Dried fruits with fresh pears is a light dessert to end any meal.

Five Fruit And Berry Compote

4-6 individual dishes.   Serves 4-6

Tea Infusion

1/2 cup water 2 tea bags (preferably English Breakfast) 3 fresh mint sprigs	Bring to a boil. Add and stir until mint is wilted. Remove from heat and cover at least 10 minutes. Set aside.

Fruits

12 strawberries 2 cups cherries 1 ripe mango 1 cup blueberries 1 cup raspberries	Prepare by removing leaves and pits. Cut into bite-size pieces. Set aside.

Syrup

2/3 cup sugar 1 tsp vanilla 1 1/2 cups dry white wine 1/2 cup port wine 1 1/2 cups water	Place in saucepan. From Tea Infusion, remove tea bags and, with fingers, gently squeeze liquid into syrup mixture.

Bring syrup to a boil and pour over prepared fruits. Return fruits to stove and bring to a simmer over high heat. Add mint sprigs from Tea Infusion and remove from heat. Place in refrigerator and chill well. Serve in soup bowls.

Any combination of favorite fruits can be used.
A great contrast to rich desserts.

Classic Crème Brûlée

Preheat oven to 325°F.
5-6 individual oven dishes.

1 1/2 cups whipping cream 1/2 cup milk 1 tbsp vanilla 1/4 cup sugar	In saucepan, combine. Stir over medium heat until sugar is dissolved. Remove from heat.
6 egg yolks 1/4 cup sugar	In separate bowl, whisk together. Add cream mixture to yolks, whisking constantly. Return to stove and cook for 1-2 minutes on a low heat stirring constantly until slightly thickened. Remove from heat. Pour into dishes. Set dishes in water bath and bake for 40-50 minutes until set. Sprinkle top of mold with 1 tsp sugar and place under broiler just until bubbly.

A rich and smooth Brûlée.

AURORA

Celestial inspiration may be responsible for Joe Baum's spectacular Aurora. The ancient Romans believed that each morning the goddess Aurora awoke from a night of dreams to present humanity with yet another glorious, rosy daybreak. This classy French bar-restaurant, named after the deity, relies on etherial decor, staff as pleasant and patient as cherubim, and out-of-this world food to transport its eclectic clientele.

Dawn brings with it a metamorphosis in the menu, assuring new and unusual creations. Once diners drift beneath a postmodern canopy, they enter a very comfortable world. A large winding bar of pink and grey granite dominates, offering the usual spirits. Floating on a Glaser-designed bubble motif carpet, patrons are coaxed by wings and pastel lights past an effigy of the reclining Aurora into a bi-sectioned dining room. In this blissful environment, divine concoctions of the haute cuisine kind are served, soothing the hungry while inspiring palates to rapture.

Desserts in such an establishment must rise above the carnal and ascend towards perfection. Expect the familiar to be laced with inventiveness: tempting Apple Tarts from the Garden of Eden, a blend of four Fresh Berries with a heady Granite of Pinot Noir and a delicate Apricot Mousse with substance. For a taste of nirvana, experiment with these heavenly delights.

Apple Tart

Preheat oven to 375°F.
8" flan pan.

Crust

3 oz butter ⎫
3/4 cup flour ⎬ Combine until dough comes
1 tbsp water ⎭ together. Form a ball. Pat thinly into pan and prebake approximately 15-20 minutes, or until light brown. Meanwhile, prepare apples. (If you have time, refrigerate unbaked dough before baking, approximately 30 minutes).

Tart

4 medium apples Peel, core and slice thinly. Arrange apples in a fan-like circle on the dough.

2 tbsp sugar Sprinkle over top apples.

1 oz butter Place small pieces over top apples. Bake for approximately 20-30 minutes, or until apples are tender. Cool and sprinkle with cinnamon and serve with ice cream.

A small, yet sophisticated tart.

Fresh Berries
with Granite of Pinot Noir

6 individual dishes. Serves 6

3/4 cup sugar } 3/4 cup water }	In saucepan, bring to a boil. Remove from stove to cool.
1/3 cup Pinot Noir wine } or substitute } Juice of 1 orange } Juice of 1 lemon }	Add to cooled syrup. Mix well. Transfer to shallow pan and freeze, stirring once an hour with a fork to break up frozen layers. Repeat when granite has reached a consistency similar to ice shav- ings, approximately 2–3 hours.
1/4 lb strawberries } 1/4 lb blueberries } 1/4 lb raspberries } 1/4 lb blackberries } (if available) }	Add to above granite and serve in individual dishes.

One of Aurora's lightest
and most calorie-conscious desserts.

Apricot Mousse

6 cup mold.

1 1/2 cups packed apricots 1 cup water }	Simmer in saucepan on medium heat until tender. Purée. Set aside.
5 egg yolks 1/4 cup sugar }	Mix until blended. Add to apricots and mix well.
1 tsp gelatin	Dissolve according to instructions on package. Add to apricot mixture and cool.
1 1/2 cups whipping cream 2 tbsp sugar }	In clean bowl, beat until stiff. Fold into apricot mixture.
1/3 cup apricot or fruit liqueur }	Fold into entire mixture and pour into mold. Chill for at least 2–3 hours. Invert by dipping mold into hot water for a few seconds. Serve individual pieces with red current purée, if desired.

Red Currant Purée (optional)

2 cups red currants 1 cup sugar }	Purée.

A rich, dense mousse with fruity substance.

NEW YORK

Classically elegant and tastefully refined, Lafayette is a formal French dining room in New York's famous Drake Hotel. Here diners are provided the respect traditionally found in first-class European establishments.

Master chef Louis Outhier is consulting chef at Lafayette. In Europe, Outhier is famous for L'Oasis, La Napoule, on the Riviera, long one of France's elite restaurants. At Lafayette he has created a superb table d'hôte with a nod towards Southeast Asian spicing.

The dining room is large, sectioned by four columns. Above, a fabulous crystal chandelier hangs from the mirrored ceiling, which further reflects the glittering light. Below, a profusion of fragrant flowers is illuminated. In this luxurious, softly lit, subtle environment, walls covered in raw silk the color of burnt sienna, hardwood armchairs upholstered in a plush wine fabric, and virgin white tables create a decor aligned with cultivated sensibilities. But the focus at Lafayette is on what's going on behind the sound-proof window of glass. Clientele are treated to the sight of a cadre of earnest chefs scurrying about an immaculate, silvery kitchen preparing the bill of fare with *élan*.

Mango Strudel with Kiwi Sauce and Passion Fruit Mousse Cake are such tropical delights that, with eyes closed, you're sure to have visions of swaying palms and tourquoise oceans. The unusual blend of sweetness of Vanilla Pears with Cherry Sauce will inspire even the most jaded palates.

La Tulipe Cookie Cups filled with Ice Cream, page 87

Mango Strudel With Kiwi Sauce

Preheat oven to 400°F.
Butter and flour a cookie sheet.

2 tbsp raisins 1/4 cup hot rum }	Soak for 30 minutes.
3 mangos	Peel and cut into small cubes.
juice of 1/2 lime	Add to mango along with strained raisins.
5 sheets of filo pastry 3 tbsp melted butter }	Lay out sheets of filo. Brush each sheet with melted butter. Pile on top of each other and fill top sheet with mango mixture. Roll up in jelly roll fashion. Brush outside with melted butter. Bake until golden brown, approximately 15 minutes. Cool, sprinkle with icing sugar and serve with kiwi sauce.

Kiwi Sauce

4 kiwis	Peel and purée.
juice of 1/2 lemon 2 tbsp sugar }	Add to kiwis and continue to purée. Serve under a slice of mango strudel.

*Mangos and kiwis in a strudel crust
provide a tropical delight.*

 Espresso Chocolate Mousse Charlotte, page 90

Passion Fruit Mousse Cake

Preheat oven to 350°F.
Butter and flour an 8" springform pan.

Chocolate Sponge

4 eggs 3/4 cup sugar }	Combine and beat until thick and pale.
1/3 cup flour 2 tsp cornstarch 4 tbsp cocoa }	Sift and fold into above. Pour into pan and bake approximately 25–30 minutes, or until tester comes out dry. Cool on rack.

Passion Fruit Mousse

1/2 tbsp gelatin dissolved according to package instructions 1 tbsp brandy }	Blend and cool.
3/4 cup passion fruit juice (approx. 4 fruits)	Add to above and mix.
1 1/4 cups whipping cream 5 tbsp icing sugar }	Whip to soft peaks. Fold into above.

Assembly
        Slice cake into 2 layers. Carefully remove top half of cake.
Leave other half in springform and pour mousse mixture over top of
sponge. Grind second layer in food processor and scatter over mousse.
Chill for 2 hours. Sprinkle top with icing sugar.

*Specialty stores will carry this unusual fruit juice.
If you love the sour taste of the juice alone,
omit the icing sugar.*

Vanilla Pears With Cherry Sauce

6 individual plates.

Pears

3 pears	Peel, core and cut pears in half.
4 cups water 1/2 cup sugar 1 tbsp vanilla	Place in saucepan with pears and cook on medium heat until tender but firm. Cool. Strain. Cut each half pear into thin slices like a fan, but do not slice all the way through. Set aside.

Cherry Sauce

1/2 lb cherries	Remove pits.
1/2 tbsp honey or sugar juice of 1/4 lemon	Add to cherries and process. Strain. Serve sauce on a plate with a pear half over top. Add cherries to decorate.

Pears and cherries are great together.

LA TULIPE

At the heartbeat of Greenwich Village is a small and elegant French restaurant that, from its conception, has been successful. When John Darr, a 61 year old school administrator, and his wife, Sally, opened La Tulipe a decade ago, they felt getting started in the restaurant business at their age was an added pressure. They responded by plunging in. Sally had trained at Julia Child's school in Paris and the Cordon Bleu. In addition, the Darrs sampled recipes from around the world. Gleaning ideas, they experimented and improvised, creating their own exceptional menu. Each dish has a unique history.

La Tulipe is a cosy restaurant/bistro housed in a brownstone. Dishes are limited but varied; the concept behind each combines innovation with light sauces. Every plate on the prix fixe menu arrives looking just like a minimalist work of art.

Diners initially encounter an impeccable French ambience. A curved brick walk, edged with flowers, leads guests from the door. Café chairs accompany brass-rimmed, marble-topped tables. Posters and old menus line the walls. An exposed wood floor and wildflowers along with a zinc bar add to the charm. The more formal dining room is crowded, French fashion, with linen-covered tables. This area of plum colored walls inlaid with rectangular mirrors effectively uses brass lamps with tulip-shaped globes to create an exceptionally lively, convivial environment. French waiters serve meat and fish entrées around which are arranged crisp fresh vegetables.

One rich dessert is Tulipe Cookie cups filled with ice cream and chocolate sauce. The light and tempting Lemon Chiffon Tart cools any palate. Serve the Apricot Soufflé the way they do at La Tulipe. Present the individual soufflé to your guest, remove the cap, insert sweet whipped cream and then reassemble the fluffy structure. A sure pleaser.

Lemon Chiffon Tart

Preheat oven to 375°F.
Butter an 11" - 12" flan pan.

Crust

1 tbsp sugar
1 2/3 cups flour
6 oz butter
}
Combine until crumbly.

4 tbsp ice water
Add to above until mixture holds together and is not sticky. Add more flour if too sticky or more water if too dry. Pat into flan pan and bake approximately 20-25 minutes until light brown. Cool on rack.

Filling

6 egg yolks
1/2 cup sugar
}
Beat in bowl until pale, approximately 5 minutes.

1 cup lemon juice
(approx. 5 lemons)
5 tbsp butter
}
Stir into above, then place in saucepan over low heat stirring constantly until mixture thickens, approximately 5-10 minutes. Pour into bowl, cover and chill.

6 egg whites
In clean bowl, beat until soft peaks form.

3/4 cup sugar
1 tbsp lemon juice
}
Add to whites and beat until firm. Fold into chilled yolk mixture and pour into crust. Bake approximately 15 minutes or until puffed and golden. Cool on rack. Sift icing sugar over top when cool. Do not refrigerate.

One of the best lemon desserts ever created.

Apricot Soufflé

Preheat oven to 375°F.
Butter and sugar 8 individual soufflé dishes.

1/2 lb dried apricots 2 1/2 cups water	Soak apricots in 1 1/2 cups of the water for approximately 1 hour. Add remaining 1 cup of water and place in saucepan. Bring to a boil and cook covered for 20 minutes. Process until smooth. Strain purée.
1/2 cup sugar 2 tbsp lemon juice	Add to purée and chill in refrigerator until cool.
6 egg whites	Beat in clean bowl until soft peaks form.
1/4 cup sugar 1 tbsp lemon juice	Add to whites and beat until stiff and shiny. Slowly add 1 cup of the whites to the chilled purée, then fold back into remaining whites until combined. Pour into dishes. Bake in water bath for 30 minutes or until tops are browned. Remove from oven and sift icing sugar over the tops. Remove tops of soufflés and fill the cavities with some whipped cream, if desired. Replace tops and serve immediately.

The apricots make this sure-fire soufflé richer than most.
A heavenly dessert.

Tulipe Cookie Cups filled with Ice Cream and Chocolate Sauce

Preheat oven to 375°F.

Approx. 6 cups

Butter and flour 3 cookie sheets.

Cookie Cups

5 tbsp flour 1 cup icing sugar	Combine in food processor.
2 oz melted butter	Add and blend.
1/2 cup egg whites (approx. 3 egg whites) 3/4 tsp vanilla	Add and blend until smooth. Fill 1/8 cup with batter and pour onto cookie sheet. (One sheet will take 2 cookies). Tilt pan until batter forms two 6" rounds. Repeat on other sheets. Bake for approximately 7 minutes or until golden. Remove and, with knife, loosen one cookie and quickly place over bottom of glass or small bowl. Squeeze cookie over glass to form tulip shape. Quickly remove and repeat with each cookie.
6 large scoops of ice cream	When about to serve, place 1 large scoop or three small scoops of your choice of ice cream in center of tulip cookie and top with chocolate sauce (see page 24). Base of cookie may be brushed with some chocolate.

Various flavors of ice cream make this dessert
look like a work of art.

FRASER•MORRIS

Long before gourmet-to-go was the norm, Fraser Morris Fine Foods had been on the indefatigable search for unique ways to tantalize the palate. For half a century the discriminating tastes of New York's first families have been catered to here. Two definitive shops purvey the finest comestibles available in the United States.

Beluga Caviar, unusual cheeses, fine coffees, rare condiments and exquisite chocolates are just a fraction of the delicacies to be found. In this gourmet's idea of heaven, each shelf, every well-lit corner is devoted to attractively arranged items. Fraser Morris Fine Foods is noted for its scrupulous attention to detail. Incredibly delicious meat, fish and fruit platters are available for parties as well as the most delightful baskets and hampers filled with the perfect blend of foods. There are even Camp Baskets for kids, each complete with a cuddly teddy bear.

An entire wall is devoted to baked goods. Fraser Morris is famous for its Rice Pudding, the recipe of which is offered here, along with one for a lemon and lime meringue pie. There's also a Baked Apples with Almond Cream and, for those enamoured with the intensity of strong coffees, Espresso Chocolate Mousse Charlotte. All of these spectacular desserts are prepared by Jon-Erik Svensson.

Lemon and Lime Meringue Pie

Pie Crust (see page 26)   Bake until golden and set aside.

Pie Filling

1 cup sugar 1/3 cup cornstarch 1/4 tsp salt 1 cup water 3/4 cup lemon juice (approx. 3 lemons) 1/4 cup lime juice (approx. 1 1/2 limes)	Combine in saucepan over medium heat stirring constantly until thick. If cornstarch is still in lumps, use a beater to blend completely. Remove from heat.
4 egg yolks	Blend and add to above, stirring constantly. Place back on medium heat on stove and stir for approx. 2-4 minutes until thicker. Remove from heat.
1 tbsp butter	Add to above and blend. Pour onto crust. Set aside.

Preheat oven to 400°F.

Meringue

4 egg whites	In clean bowl beat until foamy.
1/4 cup sugar	Add and beat until stiff. Pipe or spoon meringue over filling making sure meringue touches sides of pie. Bake approx. 5 minutes until golden brown. Chill before serving.

Lemons and limes make for a classic old-fashioned pie.

Espresso Chocolate Mousse Charlotte

8" springform pan.

Approximately 2 dozen lady fingers or other fancy flat cookies	Line sides of pan with cookies and place enough on bottom to cover.
1/4 cup sugar 4 tbsp cognac or rum }	Combine in small saucepan and cook just until sugar dissolves. Do not let brown. Set aside.
5 1/2 oz semi-sweet chocolate	Melt and set aside.
2 tbsp whipping cream	Add to chocolate and stir until smooth.
1 tbsp instant espresso or regular coffee	Add to above chocolate mixture and beat until smooth. Add sugar/cognac to above and mix until well combined.
2 egg whites	Beat in clean bowl until stiff. Set aside.
2 cups whipping cream	Beat in clean bowl until soft peaks form. Fold both whites and whipping cream into chocolate mixture, just until combined. Pour into prepared pan. Chill at least 2-3 hours. Unmold and decorate with chocolate shavings, cocoa or chocolate ganache (see page 66).

Coffee and chocolate can never miss.

Fraser Morris's Famous Rice Pudding

8 individual serving dishes or one larger serving dish.

1 1/2 cups cooked rice
(approx. 1/2 cup uncooked)

Set aside in separate bowl.

2 cups whipping cream
1 egg
1/2 cup sugar
1/2 tbsp vanilla extract
1/2 cup raisins

Combine in saucepan and mix well.

Add cooked rice and cook over low-medium heat until mixture just comes to a boil, approx. 20 minutes. Remove from heat and pour into serving dishes. Cool and sprinkle with cinnamon.

One of the creamiest rice puddings ever!

Baked Apples With Almond Cream

Preheat oven to 350°F.
Oven-proof dish to hold 6 apples.

6 Rome apples

Core apples and pierce each
one 10-12 times with a fork.

2 cups brown sugar
1 cup corn syrup
(preferably dark)
1 tbsp almond extract

Place in pan and mix well.
Place apples on top of mixture.
Add water to cover the apples
half way up their sides.

1 cinnamon stick
1 small lemon cut into
6 wedges
1 clove

Add to dish. Bake until apples
are easily pierced with a fork.
Remove from oven.

Almond Cream

1 cup whipping cream
1 tsp almond extract

Whip until stiff. Serve alongside
warm apples.

An old time favorite, a bit jazzed up!

On rainy days nothing seems to distract thoughts from grey clouds and chilly weather quite so much as slipping into a charming little neighborhood pastry shop. When three cafés are operated by the same owner, it can only mean that they are extremely popular places excelling in desserts.

Les Délices Guy Pascal, named after proprietor Guy Pascal, are a trio of the tiniest and cheeriest spots in the city. Provence-style interiors feature quaint Pierre Deux tablecloths that only enhance the cosy atmosphere. On any given morning, *le petit déjeuner* may be consumed, along the lines of pecan rolls, almond croissants, Danish pasteries and the most marvelous warm brioches this side of the Provinces. Quiches, pâtés, soups and *saucissons en croute* are available for lunch and dinner. And throughout the day and evening an artful display of rich pasteries fills immaculate glass cases. Gorgeous cakes, glistening fruit tarts, chocolate mousse and delightful little cookies—everything is sinfully delicious and tempting.

One of the premier pastries Guy Pascal features is his Swiss Ganache Cake, a marvelous chocolate, liqueur and whipped cream delight. Another you'll want to create is the layered Mousse Cake combining perennial favorites—orange and chocolate. Either dessert will be a classy finish to any meal.

Orange and Chocolate Layered Mousse Cake

Preheat oven to 350°F.
Butter and flour 9" springform pan.

Sponge Genoise

3 eggs ⎫ 1/2 cup sugar ⎭	In bowl set in larger bowl containing hot water (bain-marie), beat until thick and pale, approximately 5-8 minutes.
1/4 cup flour	Fold into above and combine.
2 tbsp butter (melted)	Add and mix just until combined. Pour into pan and bake until tester comes out clean, approximately 20-25 minutes or until golden brown. Cool on rack.

Orange Mousse

2 large oranges	Grate the peel of 1 orange and place zest and squeezed juice of both oranges into a saucepan.
2/3 cup sugar	Add and bring to a boil. Remove from stove.
1 tbsp gelatin	Dissolve according to package and add to juice mixture.
2 tsp Grand Marnier	Add to above and mix well. Let cool completely.
1 1/2 cups whipping cream	In clean bowl, beat until stiff and fold into above cooled orange mixture. Place in refrigerator while preparing chocolate mousse.

Orange and Chocolate Layered
Mousse Cake
(continued)

Chocolate Mousse

6 oz semi-sweet chocolate	Melt until smooth and cool slightly.
2 cups whipping cream	Whip until stiff and fold into above.
2 tbsp Grand Marnier	Save to brush over cake layers.

Assembly

Slice cake into 2 layers. Leave one half in springform and brush some liqueur over top. Place orange mousse over top, then second layer of cake. Brush top layer with liqueur and place 2/3 of chocolate mousse over top. Chill cake and leftover mousse for at least 2 hours. Unmold and ice sides with remaining 1/3 of chocolate mousse. Decorate with icing sugar and shredded orange zest.

*The orange and chocolate flavors combine to make
this dessert exceptional.*

Swiss Ganache Cake

Preheat oven to 350°F.
Line 9" springform with buttered and floured parchment paper.

Chocolate Genoise

3 eggs 2 egg yolks 3/4 cup sugar }	Beat in bowl over another bowl of hot water (bain-marie) for 5-8 minutes until thick and pale.
1/3 cup flour 3 tbsp cocoa 1 tbsp cornstarch }	Sift and fold into above. Pour into pan and bake approximately 30 minutes or until tester comes out clean. Cool on rack.

Swiss Ganache

8 oz semi-sweet chocolate	Melt and stir until smooth.
1 1/4 cups whipping cream	Beat into above until all combined and smooth.
2 tbsp rum or chocolate liqueur	Save to brush over cakes.

Assembly

Slice cake into 2 layers. Brush bottom layer with some liqueur; pour 1/3 of ganache over this. Place second layer of cake over ganache, brush again with liqueur and top with another 1/3 of ganache filling. Chill remaining ganache just until thick enough to ice sides. Unmold springform and ice sides of cake with remaining ganache. Chill until ready to serve. Sprinkle icing sugar over top or decorate with chocolate truffles, chocolate leaves and white chocolate shavings on the sides.

The contrast of rich ganache and light genoise makes this dessert exceptional.

Swiss Ganache Cake, page 96 ▷

Miss Grimble

Miss Grimble's is a landmark in New York. Everyone who is anyone stops by eventually. This cheesecake/bakery emporium has even had praises sung by the likes of Bill Cosby and Jacqueline Kennedy Onassis.

A Manhattan housewife started it all by baking out of her home and supplying local restaurants. One of her many devotees, the famous artist Peter Max, when commissioned to design the interior of The Tin Lizzie restaurant, insisted that her scrumptious Vanilla Cheesecake be featured. In a flash of creative genius, Max christened the dessert, Miss Grimble's Famous New York Cheesecake. She went on to open her own establishment and, as they say, the rest is history.

A staggering display of mouth-watering sweets tempts and tantalizes. The array of purely sinful delights spans the possibilities, and Miss Grimble's has shared some of the best. The Apple Raisin Tart tastes like the kind Grandma baked. And the Chocolate Texas Pecan Torte has a distinctively down-home flavor. And for bakers who have always longed to try a cheesecake recipe but never quite found the courage, Miss Grimble's ABC Cheesecake is a cinch.

 Lemon and Lime Meringue Pie, page 89

Chocolate Texas Pecan Torte

Preheat oven to 350°F.
Butter and flour three 8" round cake pans.

3 cups pecans	Toast and grind one cup at a time until very fine. Set aside.
6 egg yolks	Beat until light.
1 1/2 cups sugar 3 tbsp flour 1 tsp salt 2 tbsp rum	Add to egg yolks and beat until combined. Add pecans. Set aside.
6 egg whites	Beat in clean bowl until stiff, then fold into above. Pour into pans and bake approx. 20-25 minutes or until center is dry. Cool and remove from pans.

Filling

1 cup heavy cream 4 tbsp confectioners' sugar 1 tbsp rum	Whip until stiff, then spread between cake layers and on sides of cake. Leave top layer bare. Chill.

Glaze

1 cup semi-sweet chocolate chips	Melt and cool slightly.
1/2 cup sour cream	Add to above, mix well and spread over top of cake.

*This dense pecan torte with a chocolate topping
is ever so rich and creamy.*

Miss Grimble's ABC Cheesecake

9" springform pan.
Preheat oven to 350°F.

2 cups graham cracker crumbs
4 tbsp melted butter } Combine and line bottom and sides of pan. Place in refrigerator while preparing filling.

Filling

3-8 oz packages cream cheese
1 cup sugar } Beat until smooth.

4 egg yolks
1 tsp vanilla } Add to above and blend well.

4 egg whites — Beat in clean bowl until stiff, fold into above. Pour into pan. Bake 40-50 minutes or until center is a little loose. Remove from oven. Turn oven up to 475°F.

Topping

2 cups sour cream
2 tbsp sugar
1 tsp vanilla } Combine in bowl. Spoon over cake. Bake for 5 minutes. Remove from oven and cool on rack. Refrigerate.

Simple yet elegant cheesecake!

Apple Raisin Tart

Preheat oven to 400°F.
9" - 10" springform pan or 10" removable pie pan.

Crust

1 1/2 cups flour 1/3 cup confectioners' sugar }	Combine until mixed.
6 oz butter	Add to above until combined and dough holds together in a ball. Pat into sides and bottom of pan and place in refrigerator for 10 minutes. Bake until light brown, approx. 15 minutes. Cool on rack.

Filling

6 apples	Peel, core and slice thinly. Place in large bowl.
1/2 cup raisins soaked in 3 tbsp liquor or juice, (i.e.,bourbon, calvados, apple or orange juice) 1/2 cup toasted chopped pecans 1 cup sugar 2 tbsp flour 1 tsp cinnamon 1/8 tsp nutmeg 1/4 tsp salt }	Add to apples, toss and pour into prebaked shell.
1 oz butter	Dot butter over apples.

Apple Raisin Tart
(continued)

Topping

1 cup chopped pecans
$^1/_2$ cup flour
$^1/_3$ cup brown sugar
$^1/_3$ cup white sugar
1 tbsp cinnamon

Combine all ingredients in bowl.

$^1/_2$ cup soft butter

Add to above until mixture is crumbly. Sprinkle over apples. Bake for approx. 50 minutes until apples are tender.

Apples and raisins are a great combination,
especially if you use your favorite liquor or juice.

LE BERNARDIN

Seafood is easy to overcook. But at Le Bernardin split-second timing, combined with the freshest ingredients and exquisite seasoning, creates nearly flawless dishes.

This sophisticated restaurant, offspring of a well-known Paris establishment of the same name, is a seafood lover's paradise. Diners are encouraged to blend some of the oceans' and rivers' more exotic fish with familiar crustaceans in rich courses laced with the correct touch of herbs and oils. The result is a seductively unforgettable repast. Classic bases have been lightened and the experiments, obviously successful, produce a *potpourri* of flavors—sweet, savory and salty—that titillate the palate to near ecstasy.

Delicate ivory lace curtains gracing street-side windows correctly greet arriving diners. Just indoors, a vaguely nautical-looking bar is the immediate attraction. Here, a pre-dinner drink may be consumed at one of the marble cocktail tables surrounded by plush armchairs. A clear glass and dark wood folding screen discreetly segregates the main dining area. Once guests are seated in a well-spaced environment with individual table lighting, the main room seems to come alive with vivid oils of the seascapes, docks, fish and fishermen placed strategically on blue paisley wallpaper above wood panelling. Service is formal yet friendly in this expensive setting.

The French love to take the ordinary and transform it into the extraordinary. At Le Bernardin appearance and arrangement of desserts equal the importance of taste. Here's a Fruit Soup that can start or finish a meal. Made with fresh fruit and orange cream, it is a spectacular creation no one will be able to resist. Also try the surprising taste treat of licorice and mocca as they combine in Anise Ice Cream served with Coffee Sauce. All desserts are created by the sous-chef, Dominick Cerrone.

Anise Ice Cream with Coffee Sauce

1/2 tbsp vanilla 2 cups milk 1 cup heavy cream	In saucepan, heat until just boiling.
6 egg yolks 3/4 cup sugar	In separate bowl, mix until pale. Pour some of the milk and pour back into hot saucepan. On low light, cook until thick enough to coat the back of a spoon. Do not let boil.
2 tbsp anise or licorice liqueur	Add to cooled mixture and freeze in an ice cream machine according to manufacturer's instructions. Serve with coffee sauce.

Coffee Sauce

3/4 cup milk 1/2 tsp vanilla 1 tbsp instant coffee	Simmer in saucepan for 5 minutes.
2 egg yolks 1 tbsp sugar	In separate bowl, whisk until pale and pour hot milk over egg mixture and stir. Place over double boiler, heat and stir until slightly thickened. Cool.

Licorice and coffee create an explosion of flavors.

Fruit "Soup" with Orange Cream

6 individual soup plates.

Syrup

4 cups water
2/3 cup sugar
1 tbsp vanilla
1/2 tbsp dried rosemary
1 tbsp dried chopped mint
(or 20 fresh leaves)
1/2 tsp ginger
or 10 slices of fresh ginger

Combine in saucepan and bring to a boil. Remove from heat and allow to sit for approximately 30 minutes - 1 hour. Cool, strain and refrigerate. In the meantime, prepare the fruits.

2 pears
1 mango
2 kiwis
1/2 pint strawberries
1/2 pint blueberries
3 plums
3 peaches

Peel, core, and cut into small bite-size pieces. Place in syrup and, when ready to serve, ladle into individual plates. Top with a spoonful of orange cream.

Orange Cream

1 cup heavy cream
3 tbsp instant powdered orange drink (e.g., Tang)

Whip until soft peaks are formed.

This light dessert is a wonderful finale.

JOHN CLANCY'S

John Clancy's Restaurant may serve the most reliable and tasty seafood on the east coast. New Yorkers first encountered the distinctive flavor of mesquite grilling here at Clancy's. Fish hasn't been the same since.

A century-old Greenwich Village brownstone houses this unusual seafood establishment. A feeling of elegance is unmistakable yet subdued. Downstairs dining is by candlelight in a decor of restful grays and whites. A smoky carpet lies beneath Bentwood chairs. Walls are milky brick, alive with posters of lovely spring gardens. Upstairs, dining is more intimate.

Staff here are helpful and love to offer suggestions. The menu is limited but circumspect; nothing needed is missed. This is a very American restaurant—direct, quality established—with none of the subtle vagaries often met in more European establishments.

Desserts, too, have a distinctly American feel. Any one of these will appeal: Chocolate Cream Roulade, a round of sponge cake and chocolate coffee; Bourbon Pecan Tart, a taste of the old south at its finest; Mocha Crème Brûlée for an unusual custard; or the luscious Almond Pear Cream Tart. Each one is guaranteed to encourage seconds.

Chocolate Cream Roulade

Preheat oven to 375°F.
Butter jelly roll pan 11" x 17" and line with
buttered and floured parchment paper.

Cake

8 oz semi-sweet chocolate 3 tbsp prepared strong coffee	Melt in microwave or double boiler. Set aside.
6 egg yolks 3/4 cup sugar	Beat in bowl until thickened.
1 tsp vanilla extract	Add to yolk/sugar mixture and slowly add melted chocolate. Mix until thoroughly combined.
6 egg whites	In clean bowl, beat until foamy.
1/4 cup sugar	Add to whites and beat until stiff. Fold whites into above chocolate mixture, combining completely. Pour into pan and bake 15-17 minutes until cake tester comes out dry. Cool cake on wire rack. Sprinkle top of cake with 2 tbsp cocoa. Place 2 sheets of fresh parchment paper over cake and carefully invert. Slowly peel off parchment paper. Set aside.

Filling

1 3/4 cups whipping cream 3 tbsp icing sugar	Beat until stiff.
2 tbsp cognac or chocolate liqueur	Brush top of cake with liqueur. Spread whipped cream evenly over cake. Roll cake in a jelly roll fashion with the aid of the underlying fresh parchment paper. Cake is very delicate. If it begins to break, just continue to firmly roll. Glaze will hide cracks. With 2 spatulas, transfer cake to a platter. Refrigerate while making glaze.

Chocolate Cream Roulade
(continued)

Glaze

6 oz semi-sweet chocolate ⎱
2 tbsp prepared strong coffee ⎰
3 tbsp soft butter ⎱
1 tbsp honey ⎰

Combine in small saucepan until melted. Stir until smooth. Cool before icing entire cake.

1/3 cup toasted sliced almonds

Sprinkle nuts over glaze.

Remove from refrigerator 1/2 hour before serving.

The roulade is delicate, moist and a chocolate lover's delight.

Mocha Crème Brûlée

Preheat oven to 325°F.
5 or 6 individual oven-proof dishes.

2 cups heavy cream
1 tbsp instant espresso
} Heat in saucepan, until hot, not boiling.

4 egg yolks
1/2 cup sugar
} In clean bowl, beat until well blended. Slowly beat hot cream into egg mixture.

3/4 tsp vanilla extract
1/4 cup chocolate liqueur
} Add to above, mixing well. Remove any foam from custard. Pour into dishes and place in another pan half filled with water (water bath). Cover pan loosely with foil. Bake 45-60 minutes or until lightly set. Cool. Sprinkle tops of dessert with brown sugar. Place under broiler until sugar caramelizes (1-2 minutes). Serve immediately.

The coffee flavor gives this Brulée a totally different quality.

Bourbon Pecan Tart

Preheat oven to 350°F.
11" tart pan with removable bottom.

Pastry

2 cups flour 1/2 tsp salt 1 tbsp sugar	Combine in bowl until mixed.
6 oz butter	Add to above until well combined.
1/2 cup ice water	Add to above and mix until dough holds together or ball forms. Pat into tart pan. Prebake until light brown, 20-25 minutes. Meanwhile, make filling.

Filling

1/3 cup bourbon 5 oz pecan halves	Soak pecans in bourbon, set aside.
1 1/4 cups corn syrup (preferably dark) 1 cup sugar	In saucepan, bring to boil without stirring. Remove from heat.
4 oz butter, softened	Whisk in butter. Let cool slightly.
5 eggs	In separate bowl, mix eggs until combined. Drain bourbon from pecans and add to eggs. Set pecans aside.
1 tbsp vanilla	Add to egg/bourbon. Gradually add corn syrup mixture.
5 oz pecan pieces	Spread pecans on bottom of pan. Spread bourbon-flavored pecan halves over pecan pieces. Pour corn syrup mixture carefully over top. Bake approximately 50-60 minutes, or until filling is puffed and lightly browned. Cool 2 hours before cutting.

The bourbon laces this pecan pie with deep southern comfort!

Almond Pear Cream Tart

Preheat oven to 375°F.
10" - 11" removable pie pan.

Poached Pears

4 cups water 2 cups sugar 1 tsp milk zest of 1 lemon 2 tbsp lemon juice	Combine in saucepan and bring to a boil.
6 medium pears (peeled, cored and halved)	Add to above and simmer until tender, 10-15 minutes. Cool in liquid while preparing crust.

Pastry

1 1/2 cups flour 1/3 cup icing sugar	Combine in bowl or food processor.
6 oz butter	Add to above until ball forms. Pat into pie pan and prebake for approximately 20 minutes, or until light brown. Cool on rack.

Almond Cream

4 oz almond paste 1/2 cup sugar	Beat until smooth.
4 oz soft butter	Add and beat until smooth.
2 eggs 1/2 tsp vanilla	Add and continue beating.
1/3 cup flour	Mix in flour until combined and refrigerate.

Almond Pear Cream Tart
(continued)

Assembly

      Spread almond cream over prebaked crust. Drain pear halves and slice thinly. Place over almond cream. Bake for approximately 45 minutes or until almond cream appears set. Cool on rack.

Topping

1/2 cup apply jelly	Heat until melted.
2 tbsp fruit liqueur (preferably pear)	Add to above. Spread over pears.
4 tbsp chopped nuts (optional)	Sprinkle over top.

The combination of pears and almonds
in a shortbread crust is fabulous.

Peppermint Park™

When an old-fashioned ice cream parlor with peppermint-colored walls and fifty delicious flavors of ice cream opens in Manhattan, success is inevitable. Add to this recipe light meals and interesting beverages and you've got a winner.

Peppermint Park Café and Bakery is an informal restaurant with a carnival-like atmosphere. This is a wonderfully upbeat spot for families or anyone with an active sweet tooth.

Kamel Mahmoud, premier ice cream maker and cake decorator, churns out over one hundred buckets of New York's finest ice cream each day. In addition, sherbets and sorbets are served, enormous banana splits, thick milk shakes, ten fruity flavors of yogurt plus country fresh and homey pasteries, cakes and cookies galore. You'll have a difficult time deciding which of these recipes to try first: Apple Nut Cake with Cream Cheese Glaze, Double Chocolate Chunk Cookies, Chocolate Lovers' Chocolate Sundae or Peppermint Stick Ice Cream, each popular dessert a mouth-watering extravaganza.

Apple Nut Cake
With Cream Cheese Glaze

Preheat oven to 350°F.
Butter and flour bundt pan.

1 1/2 cups sugar 1 1/4 cups vegetable oil	Combine in large bowl and mix well.
3 eggs 2 tsp vanilla 1/2 tsp cinnamon	Add to above and mix well.
1 3/4 cups flour 1 tsp baking soda 1 tsp salt	Add to above and stir until smooth. Do not overmix.
1 cup chopped walnuts 1/2 cup raisins 3 cups diced apples (approx. 2 medium apples)	Fold into above until combined. Pour into pan and bake approx. 50-60 minutes or until tester comes out dry. Cool on rack before inverting and icing.

Cream Cheese Glaze

6 oz cream cheese 1/4 cup butter 1 tsp vanilla	Beat until smooth.
2-3 cups icing sugar	Add one cup at a time until of a spreadable consistency. Ice entire cooled cake.

Apples, nuts and cream cheese are absolutely mouth-watering.

Peppermint Stick Ice Cream

One 8 oz package cream cheese
3/4 cup sugar
Beat until smooth.

1 cup milk
1 egg
Add to above until mixed.

2 cups whipping cream
1 tsp mint (extract)
Add to above and stir well. Adjust mint flavoring to taste. Freeze according to ice cream manufacturer's instructions.

1/2 cup crushed peppermint stick
Just before ice cream is frozen, add peppermint stick until combined.

Leftover Christmas candy canes make a truly unusual ice cream.

Double Chocolate Chunk Cookies

Preheat oven to 350°F.   Makes 2 dozen
Butter and flour 2 cookie sheets.

1 cup softened butter   Cream in large bowl with mixer.

1 cup sugar ⎫
1/2 cup brown sugar ⎬   Add to above until fluffy.
1 tsp vanilla ⎭

1 large egg   Beat into above.

1/3 cup cocoa ⎫   Beat into above just until
2 tbsp milk ⎭   combined.

1 3/4 cups flour ⎫   Mix into above just until blended.
1/4 tsp baking powder ⎭

6 oz semi-sweet chocolate chips ⎫
or 6 oz of a semi-sweet chocolate ⎬   Fold into above.
square cut into small chunks. ⎪
1 cup chopped walnuts ⎭

Drop by rounded teaspoonfuls
onto baking sheets. Bake for
11-13 minutes or until tester
comes out dry.

A cookie well beyond the chocolate chip.
An adult's as well as a child's ecstasy.

Chocolate Lovers' Chocolate Sundae

5 small serving dishes

5 scoops chocolate chip ice cream
5 scoops chocolate nut fudge
ice cream
5 scoops rocky road ice cream
(or any chocolate combination
you enjoy)
} Place one scoop each in individual dish.

Hot Fudge Topping

1/4 cup butter
4 oz semi-sweet chocolate
} Melt in microwave or double boiler.

1/4 cup icing sugar — Add gradually so sugar dissolves.

1/2 cup heavy cream — Add and blend well. Place over heat just until sauce is very hot and smooth.

1 tsp vanilla — Add and serve hot.

Chocolate Whipped Cream

1 cup heavy cream
1 tbsp chocolate syrup
} Whip until stiff. Top each dish with a large spoonful.

Decorate with either chocolate sprinkles or a chocolate kiss.

Out of this World!

CHALET SUISSE

An eatery that has existed for sixty-five years and maintained quality, consistency and, for nearly two of those decades, the same chef, is decidedly unusual.

Visiting the Chalet Suisse for a meal is temporarily stepping back to a simpler world. You'll find no high-tech lighting or nouvelle cuisine here. Dark wood beams, grillwork, roughened walls and tables and banquettes fit snugly into niches, creating a comfortable old-world ambience. While diners study oil paintings and Tyrolean folk crafts on display, cheerful waitresses in costumes native to Switzerland happily serve food that is both hearty and delicious.

Konrad Egli purchased Chalet Suisse from its original owners in 1953. Miraculously he's managed to keep both the original style and quality. Eighty-five per cent of his customers are repeats, understandable given his very personalized approach. The paradox is that Chalet Suisse is always full yet rarely mentioned in restaurant reviews and guide books. New Yorkers can obviously keep a secret.

Egli heaps deserved praise on executive chef, Dietmar Schlueter, who, since 1961, has turned out consistently wonderful meals and scrumptious desserts. Chocolate is a Swiss institution and the dessert menu reflects that. The Chocolate Liqueur Fondue for two is creamy and sharply-sweet. Into this heavenly concoction dip slices of pineapple, banana and apple to create hot little candies. As well there's a divine meringue sweet called Chocolate Dacquoise Layered with Cream and Berries, Hollander Cake filled with marzipan and a classic Bread Pudding to warm every heart. Try these wonderful desserts from the land of the snow-capped Alps where they understand the essence of good eating.

Chocolate Dacquoise Layered with Cream and Berries

Preheat oven to 275°F.
Line 3 cookie sheets with buttered and floured parchment paper.
Outline three 8" circles on paper.

Chocolate Meringue

(6-7 eggs) 1 cup egg whites 1 3/4 cups sugar	Beat whites in clean bowl with 1/4 cup sugar. Beat until almost firm. Continue beating while slowly adding the other 1 1/2 cups sugar. Beat until all sugar is incorporated.
4 oz semi-sweet chocolate	Melt in clean bowl and when smooth, carefully fold into above. With pastry bag, outline the 3 circles with meringue. (Use decorating tube or spoon). Bake for 1 1/2 hours or just until crisp and golden. Rotate meringues in oven if one begins to brown too much. Cool on rack and carefully peel off paper. Meringue top may crack slightly.

Filling

2 1/2 cups whipping cream 1/2 cup icing sugar	Beat until stiff. Set aside.
1 pint strawberries	Slice, set aside.

Assembly

Place 1 meringue layer on dish, spoon some whipped cream and strawberries over top. Repeat with other 2 meringue layers. Top with whipping cream and decorate with strawberries.

Chocolate meringue, strawberries and cream are
too delicious and beautiful to be true.

Hollander Cake

Preheat oven to 375°F.
Butter 8" - 9" springform pan.

Crust

3/4 cup flour 1/3 cup icing sugar	Combine.
3 oz butter	Add until dough comes together. Pat into bottom of pan. Bake for 15-20 minutes, just until golden brown.
2 tbsp raspberry jam	Cool on rack and then spread some raspberry jam over crust.

Cake

5 1/2 oz butter 1/3 cup sugar	Blend until smooth.
1 egg yolk	Add and mix until combined.
7 oz softened almond paste 4 eggs	Alternately add to above butter mixture, beating after each addition.
1 tsp lemon juice	Add and mix well.
1 cup flour 1 tbsp baking powder	Fold into above, until combined. Pour into pan and bake approximately 40 minutes or until center remains a little loose. Cover with foil if top browns too quickly. Cool on rack. Decorate with icing sugar.

A marzipan lover's paradise.

Swiss Chocolate Fondue

Serves 4

3 oz milk chocolate 3 oz semi-sweet chocolate }	Melt and stir until smooth.
1/2 cup heavy cream (warmed)	Add and mix well.
1 tsp cognac, or kirsch, or rum	Stir into above. Keep chocolate warm over fondue set, double boiler, or within a microwave.

Dipping Fruits

Mandarin orange sections, pineapple chunks, apple, banana and strawberries.

What a fun evening!

Classic Bread Pudding

Preheat oven to 350°F.
Butter and flour 8" rectangular pan.

1 cup raisins soaked in water or rum	Set aside.
4 oz french bread or 3 thinly sliced rolls (day old)	Toast lightly.
2 cups light cream 4 egg yolks 5 tbsp sugar 1 tsp vanilla	Combine in large bowl and stir well.
1/2 apple	Peel, core and slice thinly.
1/2 cup chopped nuts	Add apple slices, nuts, and drained raisins to cream mixture. Add bread. Let stand 2 minutes, and stir well. Pour into cake pan.
1 1/2 oz butter	Cut and sprinkle over bread mixture. Bake in a water bath for approximately 30 minutes. Remove water bath and bake 15 minutes more. Refrigerate. Sprinkle icing sugar over top. Serve with vanilla sauce.

Vanilla Sauce

1 cup milk 1 tbsp vanilla	Bring to a boil in a saucepan. Lower heat.
3 egg yolks 1/3 cup sugar	In clean bowl beat until pale. Pour the above milk mixture into yolks and stir until combined. Pour entire mixture back into saucepan and on low heat stir until mixture coats back of spoon. Do not let mixture boil. Remove from heat and cool.

An old-time favorite.

...since 1892

There's an Italian coffee/bake shop/grocery store located in Little Italy that's been going strong since 1892. Ferrara is known throughout Manhattan for freshness and goodness. Behind its deserved success is a fascinating story.

Antonio Ferrara was an opera impresario and showman at the end of the last century. He, with his buddy, Enrico Scoppa, got it into their heads to open a little café where they and other opera buffs from the old country could play Neapolitan card games and linger over strong cups of coffee after a performance. Friends like the famous Caruso sang the praises of their pastries.

Then the depression hit. Ferrara's nephew stowed away on a boat to New York, wed Scoppa's daughter and eventually the couple took over the business, living above the store. During tough times, baking was done in small batches throughout the day. Soon rumors flew throughout the city that you could pop into Ferrara anytime and find something just coming out of the ovens.

Today, still family owned and operated, Ferrara has changed very little. It's a charming café that serves hot and cold drinks, ice cream, gelati, Italian cakes and tortes and light lunches.

Of the many old-world style desserts available, Ferrara offers some of its most popular. Everybody loves cream puffs. Try Cream Puffs with Cannoli filling; the flavor is unusual. Almond Ricotta Cheesecake is a light cheesecake with an exceptionally creamy texture and delicate almond taste. *Delizioso*!

Cream Puffs with Cannoli Filling and Chocolate Sauce

Preheat oven to 400°F.
Butter and flour cookie sheet.

Makes approx. 16-18 puffs.

Cream Puffs

1/2 cup water 1/2 tsp salt 2 oz butter	Put in saucepan and bring to a boil. Remove from heat.
1/2 cup flour	Add, mixing well. Bring back to a medium heat, stirring vigorously for a minute or two until pastry comes away from saucepan. Remove from heat, stirring vigorously again.
3 medium eggs	Add one at a time and whisk until combined. Spoon or pipe mixture onto cookie sheet in the size of walnuts. Sprinkle with some sugar and bake until golden brown, approximately 20-25 minutes. Do not open door for the first 15 minutes. Cool on rack.

Filling

2 cups ricotta cheese 2/3 cup icing sugar	Beat well until smooth.
3 oz semi-sweet chocolate chips 2 tbsp diced candied fruit (optional) dash of cinnamon	Add to above and mix well. Refrigerate for 10 minutes. Cut a small hole in bottom of cream puff and place 2 tsp of filling in each. Place on serving dish. Serve with chocolate sauce. (see page 24).

Ricotta cheese and chocolate give these cream puffs
a unique quality!

Almond Ricotta Cheesecake

Preheat oven to 375°F.
9" springform.

Crust

1 cup butter	Cut into small pieces. Place in large bowl.
1 cup sugar	Add and beat until creamy.
2 cups flour 9 oz ground almonds 1/2 tsp cinnamon	Add to above until mixture becomes crumbly.
2 egg yolks	Combine with above until mixture holds together. Save 1/3 of mixture for topping. Pat remainder onto sides and into bottom of pan. Refrigerate springform.

Filling

3 cups ricotta cheese (1 1/2 lbs) 1/3 cup sugar	Beat until smooth.
4 egg yolks 1/2 tsp almond extract	Add to above and mix until blended.
4 egg whites	Beat in clean bowl until stiff and fold into above. Pour into crust. Crumble remaining 1/3 of crust mixture on top. Bake for 50-60 minutes or just until tester comes out barely dry. Let pie cool in oven with door open, then cool further on rack. Refrigerate and dust with icing sugar.

Lighter and creamier than all other cheesecakes!

Francine Gindi's career as a pastry chef has led her to some of the best restaurants in the city. When she opened Gindi in 1982, her desserts were already so popular that the shop was greeted with rave reviews from every food critic in town.

Gindi admits that it may sound corny, but her ambition was to create a comfortable working environment where people could work together creating desserts they could feel good about. This is just what she's done.

Located on Broadway near the home of the original Madison Square Gardens, this bake shop consistently turns out simple yet flavorful pastries. The front of the store is devoted to displaying baked goods and at the back are tables and chairs for consuming the desserts on the premises. Pies are excellent, warm with flaky crusts. Try the Chocolate Pecan Pie or Sour Cream Apple Pie. For a fancier dessert, try the elaborately delicious Chocolate Truffle Cake.

Chocolate and Coffee Truffle Cake

Preheat oven to 350°F.
Butter and flour 10" springform pan.

16 oz chocolate 1/2 cup prepared strong coffee	Melt and stir until smooth. Set aside.
6 eggs 1/2 cup sugar	In separate bowl, beat until light. Fold in above chocolate mixture until blended.
1 cup heavy cream	Whip until stiff. Fold into above. Pour into pan, and bake for approximately 50 minutes, just until center is no longer loose. Refrigerate until cold. Sprinkle icing sugar over top.

The easiest yet most delicious chocolate dessert ever.

Chocolate Pecan Pie

Preheat oven to 350°F.
9" - 10" buttered flan pan.

Crust

1 1/2 cups flour 1/3 cup icing sugar }	Combine in food processor.
6 oz butter	Add until ball forms. Pat into bottom and sides of pan. Bake approximately 15-20 minutes until slightly brown. Cool.

Pie

3 oz semi-sweet chocolate 1 oz butter }	Melt and stir until smooth. Set aside.
1 cup corn syrup 1 cup sugar }	Heat until easy to mix. Add chocolate mixture and blend well.
3 eggs	Add to above until combined.
1 cup pecan halves 1/4 cup small semi-sweet chocolate chips (optional) }	Add and combine. Pour into crust and bake approximately 45 minutes or until center remains a little loose. Cool.

Pecans and chocolate have always been great together.

Sour Cream Apple Pie

Preheat oven to 350°F.
Butter and flour 9" pie pan or springform pan.

Crust

1 1/2 cups graham cracker crumbs
1/2 cup melted butter
1/4 cup sugar

Combine well and press into pan. Refrigerate.

Filling

3/4 cup sugar
2 tbsp flour
1 cup sour cream
1 egg
1 tsp vanilla
1/4 tsp cinnamon

Mix in large bowl until well combined.

5 large apples

Peel, core and slice thinly. Add to above and mix well. Pour into crust and bake 30 minutes. Meanwhile, prepare topping.

Topping

3 oz chopped walnuts
1/2 cup sugar
1/2 tsp vanilla
1/2 tsp cinnamon
4 oz butter
1 1/2 cups flour

Combine in food processor just until crumbly. After filling, bake for 30 minutes; sprinkle topping over apple mixture and bake another 15-20 minutes. Cool on rack.

With apples, sour cream and a crispy topping, you'll never want plain apple pie again.

Almond Pear Cream Tart, page 110 ▷

Sarabeth's Kitchen

Sarabeth's Kitchen is like grandma's country kitchen. But instead of being located out in the heartland of America, these two old-fashioned, homey shops are tucked away in bustling Manhattan.

Simplicity in all things is Sarabeth Levine's creed. She's owner, pastry chef and manager of the small, thriving restaurant/bakeries that produce everything from basic muffins to fancy cakes. There's a non-commercial feel to Sarabeth's as if, instead of a retail establishment, customers had wandered into someone's home. The scent of baked goods wafts through the air. Jars and bottles of homemade jams and jellies entice, spreads so popular that they are sold wholesale and shoppers can now find Sarabeth's products in over four hundred stores. It's obvious that customers return to Sarabeth's Kitchen for more than the delicious treats awaiting them. The sense of American nostalgia is prevalent, sinking right to the roots of what made this country great.

For breakfast, try Sarabeth's recipe for Scones, those delicious hot biscuits our ancestors baked at Plymouth Rock. Or Rugelach, a Jewish treat of bite-sized pastries filled with fruits and nuts. Chocolate Chip Almond Cookies take everybody's favorite one step further on the road to delicious.

 Chocolate Pecan Pie, page 127

Rugelach

Preheat oven to 350°F.   16 rugelach
Butter 1 cookie sheet.

4 oz butter 4 oz cream cheese	Beat until smooth and creamy.
1 tbsp sugar 1/4 tsp vanilla	Beat into above until blended.
1 1/4 cups flour	Add slowly and beat just until blended. Do not overbeat. Place dough on floured surface and knead for 10 seconds. Divide into 2 parts . Refrigerate about 30 minutes. Roll out 1 part of dough into a circle approximately 1/8" thickness. Repeat with other half.

Filling

1/2 cup jam (plum or raspberry preferred)	Spread both circles with jam.
1/4 cup sugar 1 tbsp cinnamon	Mix together. Sprinkle over doughs.
1/2 cup finely chopped walnuts 1/3 cup dried currants	Sprinkle over cinnamon mixture.
	Cut dough circles into 4 even quarters. Cut each quarter into 2 wedges. Roll up each wedge starting from wide edge to make a crescent. Place crescent on baking sheet. Bake until lightly browned, about 20 minutes. Remove from baking sheet and cool on wire racks. Sift with confectioners' sugar.

*Only Sarabeth can produce
one of the best rugelach recipes ever developed.*

Chocolate Chip Almond Cookies

Preheat oven to 350°F.   30 cookies
Grease 2 cookie sheets.

1 cup butter 3/4 cup brown sugar 3/4 cup granulated sugar	Cream until fluffy.
2 eggs	Add one at a time, beating until mixed.
1/2 tsp vanilla	Add to above.
1 3/4 cups flour 1 tsp baking soda 3/4 tsp salt	Add to above mixture and beat just until blended. Do not overmix.
1 cup sliced toasted almonds 2 cups semi-sweet chocolate chips	Fold into above, just until combined.
	Drop batter by well-rounded tbsp onto prepared cookie sheets. Bake about 15-20 minutes or until cookies are lightly browned. Place cookie sheet on rack to cool.

Almonds with chocolate chips produce a truly unusual cookie.

Sarabeth's Scones

Preheat oven to 350°F.
Butter and flour 1 cookie sheet.

Makes approx. 10 scones

1 1/2 cups flour pinch of salt 1/2 tbsp sugar 1/2 tbsp baking powder	Blend just until mixed.
1/4 cup cold butter	Beat into above just until you can see only small chips of butter.
1/2 cup currants	Add to above just until combined.
1 egg 1/2 cup milk	Beat in separate bowl and add to above flour mixture. Stir just until smooth. Roll into 2"–3" scones. Place on cookie sheet.
1 egg 1 tbsp milk	Mix and brush over scones. Bake for about 20 minutes or just until golden.

Fabulous breakfast or tea snack.
Serve with sweet butter and preserves!

Between the Bread

Between The Bread and Café Between The Bread are two immaculate eateries that, on a daily basis, delight Manhattan residents. Nowhere in this city are meats, vegetables and dairy products presented in so appetizing a manner. Food looks as it was naturally meant to look: basically delicious.

These two unique *charcuteries* —this French word for delicatessen implies heady and tasty morsels, carefully prepared—serve an impressive range of salads, sandwiches and specials. Dishes appeal to the eye, tantalize the taste buds, incite the olfactory nerve to waves of pleasure and, as an added bonus, are obviously healthy. All this and sane prices too.

A selection of homey and old-fashioned desserts ranges from a crunchy yet melt-in-your-mouth luscious Walnut Lemon Butter Tart through an unusual but wholesome Pear and Puff Pastry Tart all the way to the irresistible Chocolate Hazelnut Cake.

Walnut Lemon Butter Tart

Preheat oven to 350°F.
11" removable flan ring pan.

Walnut Lemon Butter Tart

1 cup walnuts 1/2 cup pastry flour	Grind until fine. Set aside.
4 oz butter 1/4 cup sugar	Cream until blended.
1 cup pastry flour	Add to butter mixture. Add walnut mixture and just combine.
1 small egg 1 small egg yolk	Add to above until dough comes together. Press into flan ring and chill briefly, approximately 30 minutes. Bake approximately 20-30 minutes, just until lightly browned. Cool on rack.

Lemon Butter Filling

1 1/4 cups sugar 4 large eggs 4 large egg yolks 1/2 cup lemon juice (approximately 2 large) zest of 2 lemons 2 tsp vanilla	Combine in saucepan. Beat until smooth.
10 oz butter	Melt and add to above. Beat over low-medium heat until mixture thickens, approximately 5 minutes. Do not boil or eggs will curdle. Turn heat to low and beat 1-2 more minutes. Pour into prebaked shell. Chill before serving. Decorate with icing sugar and finely chopped walnuts.

Walnuts and a creamy lemon filling melt in your mouth.

Pear and Puff Pastry Tart

Preheat oven to 375°F.
Butter and flour cookie sheet.

Puff Pastry

Use 12 oz of frozen prepared puff pastry.	Roll 3/4 of dough to 1/4" thickness and shape an approximate 10" x 8" rectangle. Reserve some dough and form a 1" high border around the rectangle. Adhere borders by slightly wetting dough with water. Set aside.

Pear Filling

5 Bartlett pears	Peel, core and cut in half. Chop 4 pears fine. Set aside one pear for decoration.
3 tbsp butter	Melt in saucepan.
1/3 cup sugar 2 tsp lemon zest 1/2 tsp vanilla 1 tsp cinnamon	Add to butter and toss in chopped pears. Cook uncovered over medium heat for approximately 15 minutes or until most of the juice evaporates. Mound in above pastry shell. Slice remaining pear thinly and arrange on top. Bake for 15 minutes. Turn oven temperature down to 325°F and bake another 20 minutes, or until bottom and sides are lightly brown. Serve warm or at room temperature with vanilla ice cream.

Light puff pastry with buttery pears is a great finale to any meal.

Chocolate Hazelnut Cake

Preheat oven to 350°F.
Butter and flour 8" springform.
Butter and flour 1 cookie sheet, or another 8" or 9" springform.

Hazelnut Cookie Dough

1/2 cup hazelnuts } 1/2 cup flour }	Grind until fine. Set aside.
2 1/2 oz butter } 1/3 cup sugar }	Cream until smooth. Add ground hazelnuts, mix until smooth. If too wet add more flour. Roll out to 8" circle or pat into bottom of second springform pan or cookie sheet. Bake for about 15 minutes, or until light brown. Set aside.

Chocolate Sponge Cake

3 egg yolks } 1/4 cup sugar }	Beat about 2 minutes until light in color.
1 tsp vanilla	Add and blend.
1 1/2 tsp cocoa } 1 tbsp flour }	Sift and fold into above.
3 egg whites	Whip until soft peaks form.
1/4 cup sugar	Beat into whites until stiff. Fold quickly into above. Pour into first springform pan. Bake approximately 20 minutes or until tester comes out clean. Cool on rack.

Chocolate Hazelnut Cake
(continued)

Mousse Filling

10 oz semi-sweet chocolate	Melt and set aside.
1 egg yolk	Beat until light.
2 tbsp butter (melted) 1/4 cup Frangelico liqueur or other nut liqueur	Add to yolk and melted chocolate. Mix until well combined. Set aside.
3/4 cup heavy cream 2 tbsp icing sugar	Beat until stiff. Set aside.
2 egg whites	In clean bowl, beat until stiff. Alternately fold whites and cream into above chocolate mixture. Place in refrigerator to chill before assembly.

Glaze

8 oz semi-sweet chocolate	Melt, stir until smooth.
4 oz whipping cream	Add and stir until well blended. Chill.

Assembly

With cookie dough as the base, place 1/3 mousse over top. Slice chocolate sponge in 2 layers and place one sponge layer over top of mousse and place another 1/3 mousse over top of sponge. Place second sponge layer over top and thinly frost cake with remaining mousse. Chill at least 1 hour. Unmold springform and cover entire cake with glaze. Slightly reheat glaze if too thick to glaze. Decorate with sliced hazelnuts and icing sugar.

Cookie crust, mousse filling and a chocolate genoise
is a triple delicacy.

Index